What's in it for me?

What's in it for me?

A Marketer's Guide to Establishing an Equal Partnership With Customers

Robin Woods

amacom
American Management Association
New York • Atlanta • Boston • Chicago • Kansas City • San Francisco • Washington, D.C.
Brussels • Toronto • Mexico City

*)ok is available at a special
discount when ordered in bulk quantities.
For information, contact Special Sales Department,
AMACOM, a division of American Management Association,
135 West 50th Street, New York, NY 10020.*

*This publication is designed to provide accurate and authoritative
information in regard to the subject matter covered. It is sold with
the understanding that the publisher is not engaged in rendering legal,
accounting, or other professional service. If legal advice or other
expert assistance is required, the services of a competent professional
person should be sought.*

Library of Congress Cataloging-in-Publication Data

Woods, Robin (Robin Stephen)
    *What's in it for me? : a marketer's guide to establishing an
equal partnership with customers / Robin Woods.*
        p.   cm.
    Includes index.
    ISBN 0-8144-5147-0
    *1. Marketing.   2. Brand name products—Marketing.   3. Con-
sumers' preferences.   4. Motivation research (Marketing)   I. Title.*
HF5416.W673   1993
658.8'343—dc20   *92-42866*
                                                        CIP

Printing number

10 9 8 7 6 5 4 3 2 1

To
Ben W. Crow
my friend, my mentor
who lives on
through this book

Contents

Preface   ix

Acknowledgments   xv

 1 What's In It For You—The Reader?   1
 2 What's a WIFM?   8
 3 Walking in the Customer's Shoes   32
 4 Targeting Needs, Not People   42
 5 Considering All Needs   56
 6 Brands vs. Product Classes   68
 7 Finding Product-Class WIFMs   84
 8 Finding Brand WIFMs   95
 9 Corporate WIFMs   120
10 WIFM Hunting   129
11 The Care and Feeding of WIFMs   153
12 The Importance of Proximity   183

Index   201

Preface

What's in it for me? was motivated by a career-long quest to answer the ultimate brand-positioning question: Why do consumers select one brand over another? As I started to come to grips with this subject, I realized that marketing is a science with certain truths and principles, which, if understood and captured, could expand the horizons of our present knowledge and allow us to do a better job of marketing to our customers. *What's in it for me?* tries to capture some of the principles I have uncovered, in the hope that it will be a starting point for discussion as well as evidence of the need for new ways of conducting empirical tests of marketing theories.

What's in it for me? started out as a short directive to a client who was having difficulty seeing beyond a single brand-positioning technique. It just kept growing over the years as different brand-positioning techniques were examined, tested, and found wanting. Further time was spent developing new positioning techniques and testing the ideas with my clients. What emerged was a whole new way of looking at brand positioning. The "What's in it for me" (WIFM) system of marketing forces marketers to approach their jobs through the eyes of the customer—to walk in the customer's shoes for a while and try to solve marketing problems from the customer's perspective. I have concluded that this is the only way to answer the ultimate brand-positioning question.

Most marketing books start with an implicit assumption that what is in this book is well understood. Then they go on to treat loftier subjects, assuming that the ground rules are fixed and

everyone uses them. Unfortunately, in today's marketing environment it is painfully obvious (especially in TV commercials)
that many marketers have lost sight of the basic principles of
brand positioning and have made it more difficult, not easier, for
consumers to buy products and services. The WIFM principles
are simple, foundational building blocks that should be the basis
of every marketer's training before assuming even that first job
as assistant brand manager.

Other books on the subject of brand positioning have focused on one strategy and tried to apply it to all brands in all
situations. For example, the Badge Theory/Brand Personality
strategy argues that brands have personalities and that consumers wear the brands like badges to show people who they really
are or aspire to be. The Marketing Warfare strategy, outlined by
Ries and Trout in their excellent book of the same name, argues
that "the true nature of marketing today is not serving the
customer; it is outwitting, outflanking and outfighting your
competitors."

Badge Theory/Brand Personality Theory, Marketing Warfare,
and other brand-positioning techniques such as Unique Selling
Propositions (USPs) and the Basic Stance have a solid place in
brand positioning. However, in trying to use them, I have
discovered that they work in only a limited number of situations.
They give you part of the answer to why consumers select one
brand over another, but not the whole answer.

The "What's in it for me" system recognizes the legitimacy
of the other positioning strategies. However, it adds new brand-
positioning strategies to the mix and then pulls all these strategies into one system or framework that tells the marketer when
(and when not) to use the various positioning techniques. Specifically, WIFM shows marketers the pitfalls of using the most
commonly used (and abused) positioning technique—Badge
Theory—in too wide an arena. In short, WIFM can be thought of
as a framework for the entire subject of brand positioning,
because it starts and ends with the reason marketing and brands
exist—to meet customer wants and needs.

To date, the "What's in it for me" system of brand positioning
has worked extremely well in the following so-called image
categories: beer, wine, spirits, soft drinks, bottled water, sham-

poos, and wine coolers. This is a tough marketing arena that relies as much or more on intangibles as tangibles to persuade consumers to buy. It has also worked well in several packaged-goods categories such as pasta and cereals. The system has also been used with great success to help a newspaper, a doughnut retailer, a gasoline retailer, a manufacturer of industrial components, a supplier of spices and ingredients to the food industry, and a government services agency arrive at positioning strategies. The examples provided in the book show that this system also works well for numerous other types of businesses, including automobiles, moisturizing creams, bathroom cleansers, peanut butter, ceiling fans, food wraps, cat litter, sandwich fillers, computers, dishwashing detergents, cheeses, carpets, motorcycles, automobile tires, mascara, cotton swabs, and even travel services. I have been fortunate over the years to have had the opportunity to test the application of the WIFM system to the development of many new brands and can report a hit rate significantly better than the industry average.

What's in it for me? is a very personal book written in a very personal style, largely because most of the content has been self-taught through trial and error. If the truth be known, what I was taught about brand positioning in school and by other marketers was incomplete, especially for someone trying to earn a living by specializing in positioning. Many years of testing and retesting the "What's in it for me" system have demonstrated to me that the brand-positioning techniques used today have limitations that marketers must be aware of.

I have also learned from my clients that because we have been taught so many theories contrary to what is written here, you may have to put the WIFM system into practice before uncovering its power. One client read an earlier version of this book twice and still had trouble believing some of the principles. It wasn't until we used the system to develop a new brand for him that he became an advocate of the system.

To my knowledge, there are only two schools of business teaching the WIFM system of brand positioning. Therefore, there are very few references in this book to studies in the field or marketing textbooks. In fact, most of the source material for this book was obtained from my own consulting work with clients or lessons I learned from my own mistakes as a marketer.

There are very few studies that either support or refute what has been written here. The marketing literature consists of many studies of marketing phenomena that examine how marketers currently apply their trade, as if that's the only way to do it. They draw conclusions based on that erroneous assumption, which eventually become marketing "truisms." I have also found that most studies of brand positioning, especially those that promote the use of intangible reasons for brand selection (for example, life-styles, personalities, occasions-for-use, and emotions), do not clearly distinguish between product categories or classes and brands. Indeed, most studies on the subject of motivational research interchange brands and product classes with such regularity that it not only invalidates a lot of the good work that has been done but contributes to heightened confusion among today's marketers about the proper use of consumer psychology and brand personalities in marketing. My hope is that this book will clear up the confusion and provide a launching pad for revising some of our marketing "truisms."

If you are interested in getting back to the fundamentals, this book will help. In fact, even if you think you have a good understanding of the fundamentals, you will likely gain new insights from this book. If you don't do anything else, please take the time to understand the difference between product classes and brands. The confusion on this subject is the single largest contributor to the mispositioning of so many of today's brands. Knowing the difference between product classes and brands may be the difference between having a solid, customer-based brand strategy and having no brand strategy at all.

My one hope is that the ideas presented in this book will be used by young people who are just learning the business; by clients to give their advertising agencies clearer directions for creating advertising; by advertising "suits" when they challenge their creative people to communicate the client's brand position more concisely; by brand managers when they are trying to figure out why the consumer should buy their brands over a competitor's; and by senior executives as they think about strategic issues and how to provide better products and services to consumers.

I have used many examples, particularly automobiles and beverages, to illustrate the points being made. To me these markets are good illustrations of the principles of competition, and their use provides a certain amount of continuity. They are also well known to most marketers because they receive so much attention in trade publications and the popular press. But most of all, I used these two industries because my own clients have told me that they can be more objective about a subject and are more likely to come up with solutions to their problems if they can get outside their own industries for a while.

In the examples I use, sometimes I praise what's been done and sometimes I point out how an advertisement could have been stronger if WIFM principles had been used. As those who have worked with me will attest, I have made some pretty big mistakes in my marketing career. But mistakes are an opportunity to learn how to do it better. So if I can pass along some new knowledge by pointing out my and others' mistakes, I will have achieved my purpose. If this book collapses the learning curve for others, I will be satisfied. If my criticisms of life-style advertising, most of which sells product classes, not brands, helps one advertiser rethink on advertising strategy, I will be happy.

But most of all, I will be satisfied when marketers are committed to solving marketing problems by walking a mile in the customer's shoes and establishing an equal partnership with consumers. After you have done this for a while, you will discover that thinking like one of your own customers brings to light incredibly creative solutions that bond customers to brands like glue.

Acknowledgments

For permission to reprint copyrighted material, grateful acknowledgment is made to the following:

- Mennen Inc. for the use of its Baby Magic ad.
- Colgate-Palmolive Canada for the Ajax cleanser ad.
- Procter & Gamble Inc. for its Jif peanut butter ad.
- Hunter Fan Company for the Hunter fan advertisement.
- Dow Chemical for its Saran Wrap ad.
- Kraft General Foods Canada for the Kraft grated parmesan, Kraft Miracle Whip salad dressing, and General Foods International Coffees ads. Kraft grated parmesan and Kraft Miracle Whip salad dressing are trademarks of Kraft Limited. General Foods International Coffees is a trademark of General Foods Inc. Kraft Limited and General Foods Inc. are companies of Kraft General Foods Canada.
- Amstrad Incorporated for its Amstrad PPC 640 portable computer advertisement.
- Lever Brothers Company for its Sunlight automatic dishwashing detergent advertisement.
- Toiletries Europa of Canada Limited for its Quorum ad.
- Meagher's Distillery Limited and James Burrough Distillers for the Beefeater London distilled dry gin advertisement.
- Golden Cat Corporation for its Kitty Litter brand advertisement.
- Geo. A. Hormel & Co. for its Not-So-Sloppy-Joe sloppy-joe sauce advertisement.
- Volvo Cars of North America for its Volvo ad.

- Corby Distilleries Limited for its Wiser's DeLuxe Canadian whisky advertisement.
- Beecham Products USA for its Oxy Clean pads ad.
- Beatrice Canada for its Colonial cookies ad.
- Chesebrough-Pond's Inc. for the Close-Up tartar-control toothpaste and Cutex Every Lash Longer mascara advertisements.
- Continental Gummi Werke AG. for the Conti ad.
- Uniroyal Goodrich Canada Inc. for the B. F. Goodrich tire advertisement.
- Cathay Pacific for its Cathay Pacific ad.
- Royal Caribbean Cruise Lines for the Royal Caribbean advertisement.
- Chesebrough-Pond's Canada Inc. for the Q-Tips ad.
- Fabergé of Canada for its Fabergé Organics shampoo ad.
- McGraw-Hill Inc. for permission to quote from *Positioning: The Battle for Your Mind*, written by Al Ries and Jack Trout and copyrighted in 1981 by McGraw-Hill Inc., and for permission to quote from *Marketing Warfare*, written by Al Ries and Jack Trout and copyrighted in 1986 by McGraw-Hill Inc.
- Maclean Hunter Limited for the copious quotes from *Marketing*.
- Dr. Robert Cooper for permission to quote from *Winning At New Products*, written by Dr. Cooper and copyrighted in 1989.
- *Markham Economist and Sun* for permission to excerpt the article on "Alive and Well."
- Crain Communications Inc. for permission to quote from their copyrighted, February 8, 1990, issue of *Advertising Age*.
- The *Washington Post* for permission to quote from the article "Car dealership fires sales force—and doubles sales," copyright 1992.

Words cannot express my thanks to my wife, Diana, who is also my publicist, for her support in making this book a reality.

1

What's In It For
You—The Reader?

What's in this book for you? Nothing if you are searching for another book on looking out for number 1, but a lot if you are a marketer who wants to do something about the current decline in consumer brand loyalty or the fact that only three in ten new brands succeed. And even more if you think there may be a better way to touch the hearts and minds of consumers and win their loyalty through long-term efforts with substance behind them.

Symptoms of a System in Need of Change

As I put myself in your shoes, I see a real need for a new system of determining and communicating brand positions. I see a serious set of problems largely driven by marketing theories that we take for granted and never question but that should be challenged because they just aren't working.

Perception of Consumers

How often have you heard your fellow marketers say that we have to find new and more subtle ways to get consumers to buy our brands? Or that consumers can't tell the difference between brands so there is no point in trying to convince them of the superiority of one brand over another? When we openly say such things, it is little wonder that both consumers and governments accuse today's advertising of portraying consumers as gullible, weak (because they need something), oversexed, suckers for flattery, easily corrupted, dishonest, lacking taste acuity, sheeplike (following the herd), and so dull that they will believe anything. Perhaps we have earned the criticism of government and consumer activists when our perspective views the consumer as *flawed*.

In this book, I start from a new, more positive perspective of the consumer as:

- Intelligent
- Interested in making life better
- An individual
- Honest
- Understanding our brands better than we do

When we walk in the customer's shoes for a while, we begin to understand that consumers have wants and needs that they are naturally seeking to fulfill. They count on us to help them fulfill these needs and will give us incredible amounts of assistance once we include them in the decision-making process.

The "What's in it for me" (WIFM) system denies the negative aspects of consumers and wins their loyalty through close cooperation, mutual respect, honesty, and sincerity. Other marketing philosophies that begin with the assumption that marketers create wants and needs rather than fulfill them set in motion an "us" versus "them" confrontation that alienates consumers from the start. In contrast, marketers who recognize the intelligence, honesty, and individuality of consumers and who have the humility to ask consumers what they want and need appeal to consumer strengths in the quest to help them get better products and brands.

In assuming a more positive view of the consumer, we enter into a partnership. The consumer says: "I'll give you a list of tangible and intangible things I want; if you provide them for me, I'll buy your brand." This benefits both parties and results in a bond that is indestructible.

In most cases consumers can't tell you directly what their wants and needs are. Therefore, a lot of what you will learn in this book is how and where to look for and apply consumer wants and needs to the development and communication of brand positions.

The Simplicity of Marketing

Another symptom pointing to the need for a new system of brand positioning is the recent suggestion that responsibility for new product development be handed back to the production and research and development people because so many new products have been dismal failures. Has our confidence as marketers dropped so far that many of us are talking openly about abandoning ship—giving our jobs to someone else? Our record of new brand development is too good to throw in the towel now. After all, who better than marketing understands consumer wants and needs? We are the gatherers and keepers of consumer information. We are the ones who talk to customers and find out what they want. We may have temporarily run out of ideas, and our success ratio may not be as good as we would like, but that is no reason to cop out and turn a marketing responsibility over to someone else.

After all, seven out of ten new product failures isn't so bad! It's merely a matter of perspective. We're batting .300, and many a ballplayer has made it into the Baseball Hall of Fame with the same average. Perhaps all we need is a new way of looking at the problem rather than a wholesale overhaul of the system.

Back to Basics

My fundamental premise is that consumers are smart and that marketers really want what's best for them. I also know that marketing isn't really as complicated as some make it out to be and that a simple, straightforward approach is often much better than a subtle or complex one.

Marketing is really very simple when you think about it. Someone invents something that people need, puts it in a package that is both attractive and easy to handle, prices it within their means, makes it convenient to purchase, and tells them it's available. If there are enough people who want the product, it will be a success. If there aren't enough, it will be a failure.

Marketing is simply caring enough about consumers to make it easier for them to buy what they need. Marketers have to figure out how a product or service meets consumers' needs and then how to make it easy for them to buy the product. It's really that simple. But with the explosion of information and the pursuit of knowledge, especially in the area of consumer psychology, has come a feeling that there is something mysterious about marketing and consumers that must be understood before we make a move. So we delve into how consumers think, react, tick, respond, and purchase; we gather reams of information so we can better understand how all this thinking, reacting, ticking, responding, and purchasing fits with our corporate philosophy and the process of making profits. Everyone becomes so choked with information and so inundated with the latest theories of marketing and consumer psychology that the simplicity of the marketing process is buried. When this occurs, we lose confidence in our abilities, and lose confidence in consumers.

But when you tear away the mountains of books and computer printouts and the hundreds of theories, marketing can be simplified into one consumer action statement: Tell me, *What's in your brand that is so superior to every other brand that I should buy it? Why does it meet my needs better than the competition?* That's What's In It For Me? or WIFM for short.

By answering the consumer's simple WIFM question, you force yourself to arrive at a brand's position by thinking as customers think—to see things from their perspective. And in doing so, you demonstrate that you care enough about current and potential customers that you want to make their buying decisions easier.

Yet somewhere along the line we turned our attention away from caring about the consumer. We started to believe that we knew more about consumers than they knew about themselves. We decided that we created needs and the consumer responded to them like Pavlov's dog. That's when marketing started to get complicated, and that's when I started to write this book. I want marketers to once again focus on consumer wants and needs, not the marketer's wants and needs. I believe that focusing on consumer needs, through the eyes of the consumer, will make marketing simple again.

At first, I didn't realize how much the WIFM concept meant to me. As I was writing this book my family became very involved in the subject. We would watch TV together and scrutinize every commercial that came on the air. We probably paid more attention to the commercials than the programs at times. Frequently, one of us would say: "What's the WIFM in that commercial?" Then we would all laugh when we had trouble finding it. This became so commonplace that it started to bother me. Each advertiser had probably spent between $200,000 and $500,000 putting pretty pictures on the air and goodness knows how much media weight. And we were laughing at them for having wasted their money.

I am committed to the WIFM idea, and I sense that others are too. In the October 5, 1987, issue of *Marketing* magazine, I read with interest an article by Paul Gottlieb, an excellent creative thinker and doer. He too was commenting about the lack of messages in today's TV commercials. He even went so far as to say (without apology) that "TV has become a reminder medium." He goes on to say: "With no new information about the product, no 'big ideas,' USPs or any other quasi-rational underpinning to count on, TV must resort to magic." Then came the line that I hope was said with tongue in cheek because it underscores the lack of confidence that is evident today in some marketing circles: "Ah yes, some (admittedly naive or worse, old-fashioned) folks have asked me: 'What does it sell?' Well, folks, commercials like these don't sell. They last!"

When I went to school we were taught that advertising had a simple purpose: to communicate something about a brand or product that would *persuade* someone to buy it. What has persuasion got to do with "lasting"? Nothing, other than to underscore a real need for a system that gets the marketer back to seeing things from the customer's perspective.

A WIFM Success Story

WIFMs have to be demonstrated to be proved. Without demonstration, a set of principles is merely a theory, not a system. Recently, I saw a presentation about how Japan's largest and most successful detergent and toiletries manufacturer achieved its success and has maintained its edge in the marketplace against such formidable competition as Procter & Gamble and Unilever. To my pleasant surprise, the Kao Soap Company has developed the number-one brand in almost every market segment it has entered by following the WIFM rules precisely and consistently.

Here's some of what is behind Kao's strategy:

- Having a corporate philosophy dedicated to the consumer, not to profitability—dedicated to "improving each citizen's health and life through better hygiene"
- Focusing on product superiority and functional differences
- Entering a new market only if Kao's product is demonstrably superior
- Positioning brands against consumer needs
- Subsegmenting business classes based on consumer needs to avoid competition between its own brands
- Maintaining a brand strategy over many years
- Using the highest quality raw materials obtainable
- Using vertical integration to ensure the highest standards of production input and output
- Striving for continual product improvement in the marketplace

Kao maintains product superiority in each market segment it enters by continually monitoring customer wants and needs through a well-developed feedback system ranging from formal surveys to pilot stores. At present, 20 percent of Kao's employees are in research and development, therefore ensuring that the company delivers on its promise to improve the life and health of its customers. Kao recently entered the cosmetics market with dire predictions from all the "experts" that Kao's "substance over style" philosophy would fail miserably in what was thought to be an almost pure "style" market. The experts were certainly surprised when Kao made significant inroads into the cosmetics market by communicating the superior benefits of its brands along with equal amounts of style.

The Kao Soap Company attests that WIFM works. However, as this company readily demonstrates, commitment to the principles of WIFM marketing is a long-term one that must pervade an organization from top to bottom. WIFM is a system that requires superiority in every phase of marketing and at every organizational level. It is a system for marketers who want to be number one in their product category. And as Kao's US$1.34 billion sales and annual 10 percent growth rate over the past ten years readily attest, the WIFM system guarantees dominant market share and superior profitability as well.

2

What's a WIFM?

What do the ads on the following pages have in common? Many things. They all show brands that are consumer favorites in their market segments. Some are soft-sell and some are hard-sell; some use tangible benefits to sell, and others use intangible benefits. Yet all have a very strong message and all give consumers good information on which to base their brand purchase decisions. The marketers of these brands realize that the essential marketing issue is to put themselves in the customer's shoes and see their brands from the customer's perspective—to see what consumers appreciate about them. They do not believe that consumers are ignorant, and they respect the consumer's intelligence enough to understand that they want to make informed purchasing decisions. None of these ads talks down to consumers or tries to pull the wool over their eyes and teach them to like their brands. But most of all, these advertisements all have a WIFM.

The Superiority Claim

Mennen's marketers probably did consumer research into why consumers use baby oil in the first place to uncover one of the problems of using baby oil—greasiness. Hence its superiority claim: . . . THE ONLY BABY OIL THAT'S NOT GREASY. Then they go on to reassure the consumer that the brand still does what baby oil (the product class) is supposed to do. So when Mennen re-

(Text continued on page 14.)

AJAX CLEANSER

COLGATE-PALMOLIVE
Ajax Cleanser
TV:30
" Clean Up Your Act."

MEN O/C: (Singing)(There are no actual words in this spot. The two men sing DA. DA. DA. throughout commercial to a tune,...

...and use showbiz...or magician type gestures to indicate the products, the stain, and the results.)

Super: Tough food stains.

DA.DA.DA's end.
SFX:SILENCE

Super: Ajax speaks louder than words.

Jif's only competition
for peanut taste.

Jif® has more fresh roasted peanut taste than any big brand.

Don't laugh. It can happen. Particularly with some of those "bargain" fans you see these days.

Of course there is a way to avoid nightmares like this. Choose a Hunter *Original*. Hunter's cast-iron construction, "oil-bath" lubrication and precision-balanced hardwood blades keep our fans running quiet as a churchmouse.

Plus our Hunter *Original* motor has a lifetime warranty.

Granted, you may pay a bit more for a Hunter. But just think how much better you'll sleep.

The Quiet Fan.

Microwave Chicken
à la cheap wrap.

Microwave Chicken
à la Saran Wrap.

By the time your meal comes out of the microwave all other wraps may have stuck to or melted all over your food.

So, unless you're partial to the taste of plastic, may we suggest you buy the one that can best take the heat.

SARAN WRAP brand plastic film is a Trademark of The Dow Chemical Company.

moved the grease it didn't remove the moisturizing, soothing, and smoothing properties of baby oil.

And the Mennen ad used the magic WIFM word *only.* In effect, the ad says, "We are the *only* ones who do this. That's why we are *superior* to our competition, and that's the single most important reason for you to buy our brand."

Ajax's WIFM is strong and very clear: "We are better than the leading brand at what every cleanser is supposed to do in the first place: REMOVE TOUGH FOOD STAINS." Utilizing the visual power of television, this highly creative ad shows Ajax's competition, in its familiar green package, without naming it. The entire ad demonstrates Ajax's superior stain-removing power, and consumers are left with little doubt about its superiority to the competition or why they should switch brands.

Jif leads in the peanut butter category because it follows the WIFM rules perfectly. Procter & Gamble's ad says: "We're superior to every other brand in the marketplace on the key sensory preference issue: PEANUT TASTE." And it does so simply and visually. Because of the universality of the taste preference issue, there is no need to show the types of people at whom the brand might be targeted. The simplicity of this ad grabs our attention. It stands out among a clutter of ads due to both its creativity and its message. There is little doubt that this ad enhances Jif's image on the taste scale and either attracts new users or reinforces the image for the already converted.

Hunter fan's WIFM is QUIETNESS, and the wide-awake eyes peering out of the darkness certainly communicate that message well. One exposure to this ad would move Hunter's image positively on two brand image scales simultaneously—quietness and quality. Good communication, good image building, and creativity all just seem to go hand in hand in good WIFM advertising.

Dow's advertisement for Saran Wrap stands out as an excellent example of a brand that has found a WIFM in a competitor's weakness: Some food wraps stick to "or melt all over your food" when food is microwaved. Saran Wrap demonstrates its WIFM with the excellent visual showing the difference between Saran Wrap and "la cheap wrap" after being microwaved. In case the consumer doesn't get turned off by the top visual, the advertiser sums up, in a highly creative way, the problem with melted plastic all over your chicken: So, UNLESS YOU'RE PARTIAL TO THE TASTE OF PLASTIC, MAY WE SUGGEST YOU BUY THE ONE THAT CAN BEST TAKE THE HEAT. It's a nice one-two punch that knocks the competition dead and tells consumers clearly why Saran Wrap is superior.

Consumer Rapport

The five ads pictured all follow the WIFM formula for telling consumers why their brands are superior to the competition. At the same time, many of these ads are visually appealing and cut through the worst kind of clutter. They are powerful ads that catch the consumer's attention and give the consumer lots to empathize with. They respect the consumer's intelligence because they say: "Here is the information you need to make an informed buying decision." In short, all these ads develop a rapport with consumers that is based on an equal partnership of mutual respect and trust. These advertisers have made the difficult job of brand selection a little bit easier. That's what WIFM marketing is all about: making the consumer's life a little easier. And these advertisers will reap the rewards at the cash register from consumers who say: "Thanks for producing products that really meet my needs, and thanks for saving me the time of comparing brands by telling me why yours is superior." That's what WIFMs are all about—superiority. And superiority cements brand loyalty.

To understand how to uncover WIFMs for your brand, you need only think of the consumer as saying, "Here is a list of the tangible and intangible things your product or service must do better than anyone else's in order to get my patronage." Only then will you get some idea of the partnership you are entering into and the payout that is in store. Sound strange? Not really! Remember, consumers are smart, and will help you if called upon. Why not give them a chance to guide you? After all, it benefits both of you.

From USPs to WIFMs

Many years ago, Rosser Reeves, an extremely clever marketer who truly had the consumer's wants and needs in mind, came up with the idea that every brand must have a Unique Selling Proposition (or USP). His idea was that a marketer's job was to define brands so that every brand stood for something different. USPs have stood the test of time well and are the platform for most of today's marketing theory.

The USP concept was developed when marketers needed to be reminded that unless the second or third brand in a product category was different from the brand leader—unique—it wouldn't sell. Clones of a successful brand offered consumers nothing they weren't already getting. Intelligent consumers would see nothing tangible in the clone to make them switch brands.

However, with market segmentation—where markets are fragmented into not two or three but twenty or thirty parts—came the problem of defining the word *unique*. Some took this to mean difference for difference's sake; others argued that uniqueness could be achieved by merely redefining the target market. Still others put forth the argument that because there is so little that is unique in brands, the marketer must find unique ways of getting the consumer to buy the brand. This latter argument takes the onus off the manufacturer to create uniqueness in its brands and places it squarely on the advertising agencies and promotion houses, which are entrusted with pulling and pushing the brand through the system.

While the debate rages, what has become patently clear is that USPs are no longer appropriate in today's multibrand environment. The USP debate just seems to push marketers away from the central issue: How do we satisfy consumer needs better? Marketers have accepted the self-fulfilling prophecy that brand loyalty is dead, and they don't even try to address the central question: How can we make them choose our brand over the others? Attention has been turned to a secondary issue: How can we better push or pull our brands through the system? The focus of attention has moved off brands that were designed to meet consumer needs and is now on the marketing tools that were designed to support the brands—not lead them.

WIFMs resolve this problem by turning the marketer's attention back to meeting consumer needs. By forcing the marketer to think like a consumer, WIFMs bring the USP theory into the 1990s. Like USPs, WIFMs say that to be successful a brand has to stand for something that is different from what every other brand in the category stands for. But WIFMs add the two missing pieces: (1) that uniqueness must meet consumer needs, and (2) that the brand must be superior to its competition on its point of uniqueness.

Whereas USPs state, "Just go out there and do something different," WIFMs say, "Go out there and do something unique," but they add, "Make sure your uniqueness is what someone wants and that at the same time the consumer can see tangible proof that your brand is superior to its competition because of this unique feature." It's a small change in emphasis perhaps, but a major change in attitude.

Non-WIFM marketers should ask themselves some honest questions: Did I spend one marketing dollar to ask people if what I have to offer is what they really want? Did I spend one advertising research dollar to ask consumers if the message I was communicating clearly demonstrated that my brand would meet their needs? Did I even think about asking my target market whether what I had to offer was superior to anyone else's offering? If the answer to these questions is no, the marketer has lost sight of consumer needs or forgotten that the brand superiority issue must revolve around characteristics that are important to the customer. That marketer has forgotten that his job is to care enough about consumers to make their decisions to buy his brand easier.

WIFMs truly are "better mousetraps" that meet tangible and intangible human needs. Today, to be different is just not good enough if the difference does not offer a benefit to the consumer.

Basic Stance Revisited

Most of us were trained in the very successful "packaged goods" manner of writing brand plans. We were taught to write a "Basic Stance" for our brand that clearly indicates what the brand stands for in the marketplace. Unfortunately, the Basic Stance is another way of saying Unique Selling Proposition, and it suffers from the same fatal flaws: The marketer never has to prove brand superiority in the eyes of the consumer, nor that the Basic Stance meets consumer needs. The brand manager and manufacturer end up *telling* consumers the benefits of the brand without even asking them for their opinion. This typical brand management manual of a package goods company illustrates what I mean:

Basic Stance

The following are a variety of attempts at clearly defining the Basic Stance:

- The Basic Stance we take in meeting consumer needs
- How we position our brand in the minds of consumers and relative to competition
- The niche we occupy in the consumer's value set
- The definition of our single most important consumer benefit
- The simple answer to the phrase "We're the ones that...."

Look at how the marketer is advised to *tell*, not *listen to*, the consumer. The real truth is, if consumers even find out your brand exists amid the tremendous amount of advertising clutter, they position a brand in their own minds, despite marketers' attempts to manipulate them. The niche a brand occupies in the consumer's value set is dictated by the consumer, not the manufacturer. The above is an example of talking *to* the consumer, not *from* the consumer's perspective—the reverse of the WIFM philosophy.

Let me show you the difference between using the USP/ Basic Stance marketing system to develop a brand position and using the WIFM system.

Suppose you are the brand manager for an auto manufacturer and your engineers have just developed the OMNIPOTENT engine—the most powerful engine that can legally be put in a car before it is declared a racer and banned to the Daytona

International Speedway. On top of that, your design people have wrapped the engine in a 1960s sports car look that reminds everyone of the 427 Ford Cobra. They've just named the car the OMNIPOTENT 1, and your job as brand manager is to write the Basic Stance. With an M.B.A. from a prestigious business school and an apprenticeship at one of the leading packaged-goods companies, you have a very good fix on what to say to the consumer. You write:

> BASIC STANCE: This car is the most powerful North American automobile on the road today.

Great stuff! Your Basic Stance meets the definition of a USP perfectly. You've captured in one succinct sentence why the consumer should buy. As you have been trained, you wrote it from the manufacturer's perspective *to* the consumer.

You show this statement to your advertising agency, which has been advertising cars for twenty years. Having just come back from the latest seminar on life-style positioning, the account executives remind you that you can't sell an automobile on the strength of its product benefit. They tell you, "a car is an extension of a person's personality, a way of expressing himself to the outside world. This is an image category. People wear their automobiles on their sleeves like a badge. We should rewrite the Basic Stance to reflect the values of the life-style segment the car will appeal to most." So they take a stab at the Basic Stance:

> BASIC STANCE: This powerful automobile will appeal to sixteen- to twenty-year-olds who wish to express their independence from the domination of their parents through their automobile purchase.

What a help the agency has been! In one sentence it has created the advertising, cast it, and set you on the road to great success with the brand. You meet your sales forecast: Kids are buying the car like crazy (indeed, parents are buying the car for their kids because they too want to be freed from them), and you are a hero. So is the agency.

But hold on! Suppose someone steps back from the project and says, "Did we really sell all the units we could have? Did we limit the car's sale by narrowing its position to too small a segment of the population? If we had put ourselves in the consumer's shoes and looked at the Basic Stance in terms of answering the consumer's superiority question, would we have sold more units?"

Let's start with the product to understand what we are dealing with. We have to find out what makes the OMNIPOTENT 1 so superior to its competition that consumers will buy it. In this case, we have a physical product we can deal with to try to understand the WIFM.

The OMNIPOTENT 1's engine is massive and capable of:

- Moving the vehicle forward at great speed
- Spinning the rubber right off the tires (making great screeching noises and creating a lot of smoke!)
- Getting a person from point A to point B in the shortest possible time
- Going so fast it takes great skill to keep the vehicle in a straight line
- Easily hurting or maiming the driver and passengers by sending them out of control at great speed.

But why on earth would anyone want something like this? What is the underlying human need for such an animal?

Looking for Consumer Needs

Basic human needs tend to flow from the very simple functional needs (for example, transportation to and from work every day) to much more sophisticated and difficult to comprehend higher-order needs.

The psychologist Abraham Maslow introduced us to a hierarchy of needs starting from the lowest level, hunger, and working through to the highest order, self-actualization. Somewhere along this continuum lies the WIFM for the OMNIPOTENT 1,

Figure 2-1. Maslow's Hierarchy of Needs.

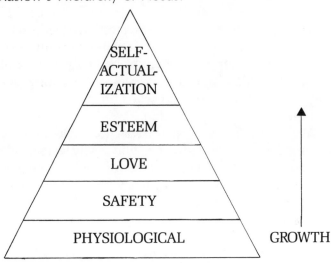

or any product category for that matter. Maslow's Hierarchy of Needs is shown in Figure 2-1.

According to Maslow, an individual progresses up the pyramid once his needs have been satisfied at a lower level. So, for example, a person who is no longer hungry or thirsty (the basic physiological needs) moves up to satisfy his need to be protected from harm (safety).

It is important to understand the definition of each of the levels in Maslow's hierarchy because, without this understanding, one cannot determine a WIFM or realize where a particular product class fits within the hierarchy.

Physiological Needs

Physiological needs are basic primitive needs for the sustenance of life itself—food and water. Without satisfying these needs, we die.

Take our OMNIPOTENT 1 example. Does it fit here? Will the consumer die if he doesn't have an OMNIPOTENT 1? The answer is an obvious no (although the manufacturer would like people to believe that they shouldn't be caught dead without one).

Safety Needs

Safety needs are second-order needs that are also quite primitive. They include the need for shelter from the elements (housing), protection from the environment (warm clothing, safety boots, umbrellas, lightning rods, and so on), plus the whole range of items designed to ward off harm from evil causes (for example, vitamins, seat belts).

Again, take our OMNIPOTENT 1 example. Does it fit here? Yes and no. No, because anyone who really wants to go as fast as the OMNIPOTENT engine can take him either doesn't give a damn about safety or has a "death wish." Yes, because many potential consumers of an OMNIPOTENT 1 reject the entire proposition at this level. They say, "The OMNIPOTENT 1 is too fast, too uncontrollable, and too unsafe for anyone to drive." Aha! Here is your first clue about the WIFM for the OMNIPOTENT 1. It may be a negative, but it is a clue and a ray of hope for eventually finding out the underlying human needs for purchasing an OMNIPOTENT 1. We have now moved from, "Why would someone want to buy an OMNIPOTENT 1," to, "Why would someone want to buy a car that is too fast, too uncontrollable, and too unsafe?"

Love Needs

Love is as far as most people ever get in their growth toward self-actualization. After all, there are more sheep than shepherds, and human beings stuck at this level tend to be followers, who are so busy looking for a sense of belonging that they gladly give up a piece of themselves to be one of the crowd. (Did you ever notice that when a family builds a house way out in the country, pretty soon they have two or three close neighbors? That's a need for love being demonstrated.)

Does the OMNIPOTENT 1 fit here? You bet it does. The underlying motivation for a portion of the population—especially the male youth group, which the advertising agency so astutely uncovered in its life-style research—is belonging and peer acceptance. To belong to a peer group, one must often overtly reject the symbols of control imposed by those in power—in this case, parents.

The OMNIPOTENT 1 fits here very well. The answer to the question posed at the second level—Why would anyone want to buy a car that was too fast, too uncontrollable, and too unsafe?—is because it is a symbol of rejection of a value system imposed by parents and a symbol of acceptance among peers. From this you can develop a large marketing opportunity and sell a lot of cars. This is what the advertising agency did in its Basic Stance.

But why stop here? So far you have uncovered only two segments—rejecters of unsafe vehicles and young males who want a symbol of rebellion against parents and acceptance among peers.

But what about postteen males? They have lots of money and they moved away from home long ago. Aren't some of them a potential market for the OMNIPOTENT 1? Of course they are. The most obvious target group are those males who never grew up. Many of them have secure, high-paying jobs and stopped worrying about their physiological and safety needs and their parents' influence long ago. What is an OMNIPOTENT 1 for them? Simple really—the same thing as for the kids. Rejection of the imposition of someone else's values on them and a symbol of acceptance among their peers. They all know that they will never be Rockefellers, and that makes them jealous and angry, so why not tell the world (their buddies) that they reject everything those old-money millionaire-types stand for by driving a car Rockefellers wouldn't be caught dead in.

But hold on: Your advertising agency told you the market was youth and has already assembled the cast for the first commercial—all people under age 21. What do you do? If you have the courage, you tell the agency that it is narrowing the target group too much by focusing on youth. You also share your marvelous revelation about the older guys who never grew up and get the agency to give you a new commercial because you've found another segment whose underlying need for buying an OMNIPOTENT 1 is the same as that of the youth segment.

If you need some forecasting data to sell management on the size of this market opportunity, the various segments can be quantified by good consumer market research techniques. But be careful of the research you buy. Market leaders and followers vary incredibly by product category. A brand leader in one

product segment may be a follower in others. It is also clear that
some product categories (such as beer and men's colognes) are
"social" products as opposed to "personal" products. For these
products, the purchase decision is a collective or group decision,
not a personal one, and sociological rather than psychological
principles apply (Maslow is psychological).

Put your money into research that is specific to your product
class rather than the broadly based psychological/sociological
measures such as the Yankelovich Survey of Consumer Attitudes. This service is good for monitoring broad general trends
among the population at large. Unfortunately, users of these
services often assume that a general population trend applies to
a specific category as well, which can be disastrous. For example, looking at today's television commercials, one would assume that almost every product needs a light/lite line extension.

Esteem Needs

Once a person has a full stomach, a roof over his head, and feels
accepted as part of the crowd, he can move up the pyramid to
satisfy higher-order needs.

Maslow breaks esteem needs into two parts: public esteem
and self-esteem. Public esteem is a desire for reputation or
prestige, status, fame and glory, for dominance, recognition,
attention, importance, and appreciation. At the public-esteem
level, the individual wants to stand out as "somebody," but the
standards used to define this specialness are essentially defined
by the masses. Donald Trump is a possible example of a person
at this level.

Does the OMNIPOTENT 1 fit here? You bet! Here are people
who desire attention, who like to dominate and look important.
Would Donald Trump buy the OMNIPOTENT 1? Emphatically yes!
But it would be a chauffeur-driven stretch version, with Connolly
leather seats, a $10,000 stereo, and twenty-seven coats of hand-
rubbed lacquer on its surface. So what's wrong with that? You
learned long ago how to segment within a segment by offering
the chassis and basic body and then selling back the transmis-
sion, wheels, seats, and so on as options. The plain, basic,

dechromed hot one with the illegal matte-finished exhaust pipes is for the kids, and the expensive, padded, fussed-up hot one with the almost illegal chrome exhaust pipes is for the older, richer "kids." But what does Donald Trump have in common with an eighteen-year-old heavy-metal enthusiast, or the guy who never grew up? What's in the OMNIPOTENT 1 for them? If we asked them, they would all probably state it the same way: "I wish I could blow every other guy off the road." In Maslow's terms, they all share a common need for a symbol to express their freedom and independence.

Kid:	Independence from parents
Never-Grew-Up-Adult:	Independence from authority
Donald Trump Type:	Independence from everyone

Now instead of one segment, we have defined three segments that appear to have a need for the OMNIPOTENT 1 and a fourth segment that has needs in an opposite direction. Are there more?

The second part of the esteem level is self-esteem. Here the person has a desire for strength, achievement, mastery, competence, confidence to face the world, independence, and freedom. This seems to be a step halfway between the public-esteem level and the next higher level. At this level the person can see that the goal is self-actualization and is driven to achieve that goal. The reference point is true self-actualization, whereas the reference point for people at the public-esteem level is the great mass of people at the love and belonging stage.

Would the self-esteemer want an OMNIPOTENT 1? Not likely. Although he shares the need for freedom and independence, it is mental freedom he is after, not the freedom one enjoys by flaunting things. We can therefore scratch the self-esteemer off our list of potential OMNIPOTENT 1 purchasers.

Self-Actualization

Self-actualization is, in essence, being true to yourself. This can take place only when a person feels accepted and safe and knows and accepts who he is. Very few people reach the self-actualization level. Self-actualization takes place when the individual feels confident enough to explore his innermost thoughts and feelings and free enough to express them and live them. A person who is true to himself:

- Drops the false fronts, masks, or social roles that are used to face life and is more truly himself
- Accepts his innermost feelings and attitudes, with a resultant feeling of unity and harmony
- Places trust in himself, realizing that he must choose and take responsibility for his own existence.
- Looks less to others for approval or disapproval, for values and standards, and for decisions and guidance.

From my vantage point, to self-actualize is to practically walk on water. Can you imagine not looking to others for approval or disapproval or for values or standards? Maslow just mentioned this final level on his hierarchy to make us all envious, didn't he? Would a self-actualized person buy an OMNIPOTENT 1? No. He really doesn't need one. He is happy with himself and is peaceful and contented. He is a gentle person who is in harmony with the world and seeks only further harmony and contentment in his life by being of service to others. In short, the OMNIPOTENT 1 would offer him nothing but noise, bother, and disharmony.

Where's the WIFM?

What we have done, to this point, is follow the brand-positioning exercise dictated by the Basic Stance/USP theory of marketing. I have taken you through this exercise to illustrate some of the pitfalls in the current state-of-the-art brand positioning that WIFMs overcome. Not that we didn't find a solid consumer-based reason to buy the OMNIPOTENT 1. We did—*but for the product class, not for a specific brand.* We forgot the most critical part: What makes our *brand* better than the competition?

Superiority

Many advertisements use the "before-and-after" formula of advertising to communicate a message. Often the advertising shows two faces. The "before" face is sad or upset or run-down, and the "after" face is up and alive and happy. What the advertiser implies is that the product caused the change and that's why you should buy that brand.

We could have used this approach with the OMNIPOTENT 1's advertising by showing a guy who wants to escape from domination. It would be very powerful advertising. You can easily see, with your mind's eye, what the TV ad would look like: The poor guy is toiling at some backbreaking job with the mean, miserable foreman hollering at him all day long. The background music is "Working on the Chain Gang" from the 1960s. The guy is clearly having a bad day, and the foreman seems to be there every time things foul up. Then the five o'clock whistle blows and the guy's personality changes as he jumps into his OMNIPOTENT 1 and peels the rubber off his tires all the way out the front gate. He either waves to the foreman as he offers the lout a big macho smile or he streaks past the foreman who is driving some beat-up jalopy.

The advertising formula of showing a before and after shot has stood the test of time and continues to communicate strongly. But sadly, most before-and-after ads do not contain a WIFM. This Miracle Whip ad is one of the few before-and-after advertisements that do.

What's the difference between the Miracle Whip ad and the OMNIPOTENT 1 ad I described? Only one copy word, *nothing*. Miracle Whip closes the door on all kinds of competition with that one lovely word. Neither mustard, nor relish, nor any other product class or brand competition can bring this sandwich to life. "Nothing" says it all!

What has the OMNIPOTENT 1 ad done to answer this question of brand superiority? Not a thing. The guy could just as easily be driving a Corvette. Communicating to consumers that the OMNIPOTENT 1 satisfies the desires of those who seek freedom from the domination of others *without tying this idea to why the OMNIPOTENT 1 is better in meeting this need than a Corvette* is the

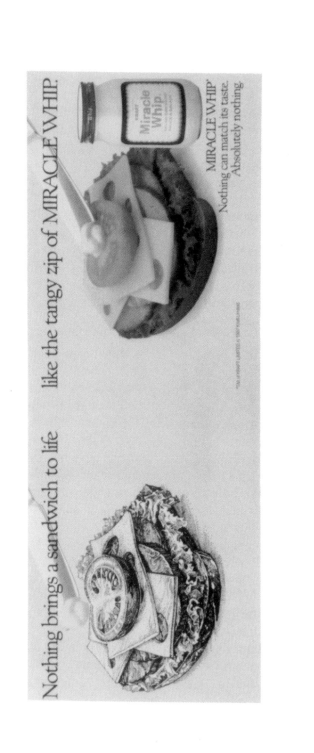

Nothing brings a sandwich to life like the tangy zip of MIRACLE WHIP.

MIRACLE WHIP
Nothing can match its taste.
Absolutely nothing.

difference between WIFM and non-WIFM marketing. The consumer could insert our competitor's name in the advertising and still walk away with the same message. In fact, the OMNIPOTENT 1 advertisement could just as easily have been a beer commercial. What happens to brand loyalty, let alone category loyalty, when that sort of substitution is allowed to happen?

The type of before-and-after advertising I just described can be seen almost any day of the week in TV ads for almost everything from beer to men's underwear. Little wonder that consumer loyalty to brands is at an all-time low when you can substitute Budweiser for Buick and walk away with the same message. Little wonder that marketers have to be reminded to go back to the basics of walking a mile in the customer's shoes to achieve an effective customer-driven brand positioning.

WIFM Basics

You know you have a brand WIFM position when:

1. It is based on consumer needs that are primary in the consumer's selection of one brand over another.
2. It tells consumers why your brand meets their needs better than every other brand that it competes against does.
3. No other brand can be substituted for your brand with the same message being taken away.
4. No other product class can be substituted for your brand with the same message being taken away.
5. It can be precisely and specifically communicated to customers.

The discovery of WIFMs is a systematic process. The steps must be followed in order without moving to the next stage until you have exhausted all the possibilities at the current stage. The WIFM steps are simple:

1. *Put yourself in the customer's shoes and see your product class and all the brands in the product class through the eyes of the consumer.*

We essentially did that in our OMNIPOTENT 1 example, except that we forgot about competition from the Corvette. Let's give ourselves half a point for this one.

2. *See all the needs, not just one or two of them. Unless you see all your customers' needs, you might miss a brand-positioning opportunity or zero in on the wrong need prematurely.* Did we see all the needs in our OMNIPOTENT 1 example? No! The agency missed the grown-up kids and the Donald Trump types and therefore narrowed the brand's target market prematurely. If the OMNIPOTENT 1 had been advertised as a car for kids, how many adults would have been inclined to buy it? Score a quarter of a point for this one, because we would have turned more than half the market off if we'd advertised only to kids.

3. *After cataloguing all the customers' needs, separate them into two piles: product-class needs and brand needs.* We completely forgot about the difference between product classes and brands. Score a zero here.

4. *Work with product-class needs first, to attempt to find a WIFM for your brand.* We did this, but we shouldn't have found a WIFM here because of the strong competition. This was our biggest mistake. Score another zero.

5. *Turn your attention to brand needs and try to position your brand based on customer needs for brands within the product class.* Most analyses will end up here because with strong competition, there are very few needs that haven't already been satisfied at the product-class level. We completely forgot this essential step: identifying needs that can be fulfilled only by the OMNIPOTENT 1 because it is superior to its competition. The OMNIPOTENT 1 brand manager was on the right track in arriving at a WIFM brand position when he initially stated, "This car is the most powerful North American automobile on the road today." Had he followed the simple WIFM rules, he would likely have arrived at the WIFM that the OMNIPOTENT 1 is the only brand to meet the consumer's need for freedom because it blows the competition right off the road in a drag race. He was, however, led astray and, unfortunately, that's another zero score for this positioning step.

So out of a possible five points we scored less than one because we didn't follow the WIFM system completely and in sequence. Only by doing so can the customer's simple WIFM question about brand superiority be answered. Only then can a strong and unbreakable bond with the customer be established.

3

Walking in the Customers' Shoes

I honestly believe that it is possible to bond with consumers. But I have only begun to understand that establishing that partnership requires a completely new mind-set in many organizations. The first step in establishing a bond with consumers is to put yourself in your customers' shoes and pretend you are a customer. Try to see the marketplace from their perspective. That's hard to do, especially for North Americans, who have often been trained to put corporate needs (e.g., management of profit to suit the optics of the stock market) ahead of consumer needs such as product excellence, price, delivery, or service.

A Customer-Oriented Approach

The concept of walking in the customers' shoes is just theoretical until you experience the practicality of doing so. A clothing store called Alive and Well recorded a 43 percent increase in sales during the recession while many of its rivals were closing their doors. The owner was quoted in the December 28, 1991, *Markham Economist and Sun* as saying, "We understand people and have the courage to do what is necessary. And what is necessary is to treat customers with trust, dignity, respect and joy. Everything we do conveys a message about how we feel about others and ourselves."

Alive and Well offers excellent products at discount prices—two musts when consumers are screaming "value." But the reason for the growth in sales, according to the owner, is the emotional plus offered customers by the considerate way they are treated. Customers leave the store feeling more important than when they arrived. This is achieved by both putting the customers in control of the buying situation and pampering them a bit along the way. Each change room in the store is sixteen square feet, with four hooks, a shelf, a stool, and a full-length mirror. "Not putting mirrors in a change room is a cheap trick designed to manipulate the customer,...and she hates you for it," observes the owner. Signs in each change room announce PLEASE TAKE AS MANY ITEMS INTO THE CHANGE ROOM AS YOU WISH. Over and above this, the store offers massage chairs, a choice of free beverages, a children's play area, baby changing tables with free diapers and diaper wipes, courtesy telephones, instant birthday celebrations for customers shopping on their birthdays, and five-dollar "Goof Bucks" if a store error necessitates a customer's return.

Alive and Well understands what it means to walk in the consumer's shoes. It understands, for example, that a shopping trip for a mother with small children can be a trying experience, and it took steps to relieve some of that stress. It understands that women like to do "touchy-feely" shopping and take their time doing it. So everything is easily accessible, plus the beverages and massage chairs tell customers to take their time and enjoy themselves. Little wonder that the store has grown so much.

The Problem of Customer Distance

Retailing is the one industry where customer distance is not a problem. In fact, it is pretty hard not to walk in the customers' shoes because retailers are so close to customers all the time. Most retailers do their market research by counting the dollars in the cash register. They can try different things and instantly measure the customer response to it. A manufacturer or a service company needs more time to evaluate the response because of the distance from the customer. This distance may explain why it is more difficult for manufacturers to think as their customers think. But there is another reason: Nonretailers are so caught up in the day-to-day business of running a company that they tend to see the company first and the customer second. A brand manager for a grocery product or a service company probably spends most of the working day thinking about the next promotion or the brand's advertising campaign or the brand's profitability. These are all company-initiated activities that have little or no bearing on what the customer wants or needs. And all this action-oriented activity leaves very little time to consider the customer. In fact, other than marketing, who else in the organization even thinks about customer needs? Do the accountants? Do the people in the personnel department? Does the president? Most presidents define their role in terms of steering the corporate ship toward a certain profit objective. That makes it extremely hard to change the corporate mind-set back to being driven by the needs of the customer.

This situation suggests that nonretail marketers, who are removed from the actual customers, will have to work a lot harder at understanding their customer's needs. Over and above this, the management of any company that wants to obtain a more customer-oriented focus will have to provide incentives to its employees for better understanding customers' needs, just as they now provide the brand manager incentives for understanding the company's need to grow and make more profit.

Customer-driven companies have to find a better balance between customer needs and corporate needs. As I said to one of my clients, "Money will flow from activities that generate a continuous flow of satisfied customers. We can't devise a strategy aimed directly at generating money. If we do, it may get in the way of satisfying customer needs."

Perhaps the Kao Soap Company philosophy of positioning 20 percent of its employees in research and development (including company test stores, test marketing, market research, and product development) gives you some idea of the lengths manufacturers will have to go to, to bridge the gap between them and their customers.

How to Tune In to Customer Needs

Once you learn to mentally put yourself in your consumers' shoes, you can redirect your thinking and the thinking of your company back to meeting consumer wants and needs, back to making it easy for consumers to select your brand.

Suppose you are a marketer of one of the new microcomputer notebooks that have become so popular. You could take the traditional marketing approach that talks to consumers from the company's point of view and list the features of the computer notebook that *you think* make it best for them: OUR BRAND IS ONLY 5.1 POUNDS, HAS PERFORMANCE, QUALITY, DEPENDABILITY AND IS JUST THE RIGHT PRICE.

However, if you, the marketer, walked in the consumers' shoes for a while and became a computer notebook purchaser, you would realize that you have to go through a lot of rigmarole dealing with salespeople, trying to sort out the features of the numerous brands in the product category and generally trying to decide whether you even need one of these newfangled gadgets or not. As you mentally digest all this information, take a look at your ad again. Wouldn't you, as a potential customer of your own brand, likely reject your own ad now that you've seen things from a new perspective? You can almost hear the consumer who has just read that ad saying, "So what!"

The reason for this reaction is that the advertisement never tells consumers why that particular brand meets their need for a computer notebook. The marketer probably never thought to ask customers what their needs were. As a result, the marketing communication is a one-way street from the manufacturer to the consumer—the marketer preaching to the consumer about how wonderful the product is. The marketer did not make the consumer buying decision easier. If anything, the buying decision was made more difficult.

If you asked them, most potential customers of a computer notebook could probably interpret the ad. *Lightweight* means that it is truly portable and easy to carry around. But *performance* could mean that it had a lot of different programs or that it performed functions quickly, or both. And so on. But the poor consumer has to do too much work to understand the benefit of the computer notebook being advertised. First she has to take the time to read all the copy, then she has to make the translation between what was said and the benefits to her. And she is still left with the nagging question about whether performance means speed or flexibility.

Given the amount of advertising a consumer is exposed to every day, there is a pretty good chance that an ad that makes the consumer work this hard will either go unnoticed or be remembered negatively. Why? Because it doesn't make the consumer's job of buying a computer notebook easier. And that's what walking in the customer's shoes attempts to avoid.

How many potential buyers of a computer notebook do you think know what this means?

20 Mhz 386SX Processor
2 MB of RAM Expandable to 8 MB
VGA Display with 32 Grey Scales
20, 40, or 60 MB Hard Drives
1Ser/1Par/1 Mouse Port
Laplink 111/Dos 3.3/Utilities

How many even have the inclination to find out? Yet ads for these types of products often contain such highly technical information. To most business executives (the primary customer for these types of products), this is a foreign language. None of it links directly back to the customer's needs without either the salesperson or the customer translating from the benefit touted to the need met.

Now think about an ad for a computer notebook with the headline OUR BRAND IS THE ONLY ONE THAT DOES THE REMEMBERING FOR YOU! Then the ad goes on to say that this computer notebook is the only one that has an alarm that goes off to remind you about important conferences. Doesn't an ad like this tell the consumer, in the consumer's language, the unique need that is met by this particular brand of computer notebook?

Doesn't the ad make the consumer's computer notebook purchasing decision easier than an ad that emphasizes "2 MB of RAM Expandable to 8MB"?

Needs vs. Benefits

As marketers, we often gloss over the difference between needs and benefits. But the difference is that needs see things from the customer's perspective, and benefits see things from the company's perspective. This may seem like hair splitting, but it makes all the difference in the world when formulating a brand-positioning statement. A quick rule of thumb is: Benefits are what companies or brands offer, and consumer needs are what those benefits satisfy.

Needs Touch People Personally

The primary reason to communicate needs—and not benefits—is that consumers' needs belong to them and them alone. Needs are personal, and by tapping into them you touch the consumer at a personal level, at an emotional level. There can be little doubt that touching consumers at a personal level leads to higher brand awareness, brand retention, and sales at the cash register. That's what needs do that benefits don't—make the message personal.

Needs Communicate More Precisely

Another reason for communicating the needs met rather than the benefits of a brand is that the communication is much more precise. When you tell consumers the benefit of a brand, the consumer has to make a translation from benefits provided to needs met. When the consumer has to make this translation, there is always the risk of the consumer getting more than one message or, worse still, the wrong message.

I discovered this while working on a project for a beverage client. We suspected that some of our rating categories in a questionnaire were being interpreted differently by respondents, so we took a sample of respondents and asked each of them to state in their own words what specific ratings meant. We were horrified to learn that the word *smooth* meant three different things: goes down the throat easily, light tasting, and well balanced. Needless to say, we changed the questionnaire to reflect these nuances.

The imprecision of the language being used in advertising is of great concern. Perhaps I am oversensitive to the issue because I am also a writer. But if advertising is supposed to persuade consumers to buy, the argument had better be communicated precisely. I have found that an advertiser can be more precise when communicating the needs met rather than the brand benefits.

Take the lite/light theme. There are so many variations that the designation lite/light no longer means lower calories or less filling, as it originally did. The lite/light label has been used by so many brands that it now means just one thing: It's healthier than the non-light variation of the brand. That may be OK for some brands, but for those that want to take advantage of the latest medical findings, it may be important that the consumer know the precise need that is being met by the brand rather than the generalization that it is healthier.

The words *environmentally friendly* run the same risk. Part of the problem is that so many marketers have rushed to get on this bandwagon that we now have everything from banks to house paint that claim to be better for the environment. When this happens consumers start to get skeptical or become so sick and tired of the issue that the words *environmentally friendly* either lose their meaning or are a complete turnoff.

It's not that consumers aren't concerned about specific environmental issues. They are extremely concerned. But when a bank tries to claim that its "Green Machines" (the brand name for its automatic teller machines) are somehow hooked to environmental issues, and when everyone and his brother are donating a portion of the money they take in to some "Save the Ozone Layer" cause, the environmental issue loses its consumer pull. Consumers start to feel that they are being either misled or manipulated or both. I experienced this response while testing a brand with an environmentally friendly feature. Several focus-group respondents stated emphatically that they had been burned so often by brands claiming to be better for the environment that they were extremely skeptical of any such claim. Virtually every respondent had some story about how such and such a brand claimed to be "ozone friendly" when it never had anything to do with the depletion of the ozone layer in the first place.

Despite this skepticism, consumers still have strong feelings about specific environmental issues such as the bulldozing of the rain forests in Brazil or overpackaging. So rather than throw yourself in with everyone else by saying your brand is "environmentally friendly," spell out precisely how your brand's specific environmental benefits meet the consumers' needs.

Consumers Don't Care As Much About the Benefits As You Do

Another reason for using needs rather than benefits to communicate to consumers is that in many cases consumers don't care as much about the benefits as you do. In other words, when you tell consumers about a brand's benefits, you may be talking to yourself.

Benefits are personal to the company or the brand manager in charge of marketing the brand. The company is proud of the fact that it developed Ultraswift or the exclusive X3TA formula, but the consumer doesn't necessarily feel the same way. To be blunt, consumers care more about themselves than about how well the company or brand is doing. In fact, if the X3TA formula doesn't meet consumers' needs, they will dump the brand without a second thought.

I experienced this problem firsthand when working on the development of a corporate brochure for one of my clients. The difference between benefits and needs became a major point of discussion. My client had written the brochure and he wanted my opinion on it. Because he really understands what WIFMs are, one of the first statements in the brochure specified why his company was superior to the competition. It read: OUR COMPANY IS THE BIGGEST IN THE INDUSTRY. This statement is absolutely true, and it expressed a tremendous pride in the achievements of company employees who had built the company up from scratch to become the industry leader in a very short time. Who wouldn't be proud of that fact? Who wouldn't want to shout it from the rooftops? As diplomatically as I could, I said, "You have every reason to be proud of the fact that your company is the largest in the business. You worked long and hard to achieve that. But do you think your clients and prospective clients are as proud of that fact as you are? Do you think they go around boasting to others that they deal with the biggest company in the industry? Let's pretend you are one of your own customers for a minute. What's in it for the customer because of the fact that you are the biggest in the industry?" Then the light went on in my client's head.

He had come from the financial services sector and was used to reading and writing corporate prospectuses, which shout the virtues of a company because, after all, they want people to buy a piece of it. That was why my client automatically thought in terms of benefits rather than needs. But when the light went on he added, "Being big means that we have outlets that are a lot more convenient for the customer to visit." So we put this in the brochure.

Then we tackled another statement he had written: WE CARRY MORE STOCK THAN ANY OF OUR NEAREST RIVALS. "What customer need does that meet?" I asked. He's a quick study, so he rapidly shot back that customers would know that when they ran short of a certain item they could be assured of getting it right away. The rest of the brochure was modified accordingly, with wholesale changes from benefits of the corporation to how these benefits met consumer needs, once my client understood that his potential customers didn't appreciate his company benefits as much as he did.

Many marketers and advertisers have trouble switching from benefits to needs and, to be honest, having been trained to think from the company's perspective, I even have trouble myself. The only way I can get in tune with needs is to pretend I am a consumer. Sometimes I do this in a different product class so I can detach myself from the issue at hand to try to bring some objectivity to the problem. Sometimes I even step out of marketing and into another business discipline to see what would happen there if I wore the customer's shoes. Try it sometime. Pretend you are the quality assurance person and think about how different quality assurance would be if it were run from the customer's perspective.

I go to all this trouble so I can get in touch with the notion that I have real live customers and potential customers who are counting on me to fulfill their needs. It's a lot of work, but as I hope I can demonstrate throughout this book, when you walk in the customers' shoes and see your marketing world from their perspective, the rewards are well worth the effort.

4

Targeting Needs, Not People

Now that you have mentally started to walk in the customers' shoes, try to see your customers not in descriptive terms but in terms of their needs. In fact, avoid the temptation to describe consumers demographically, emotionally, or personality-wise at this stage. The reason for this will become clearer as you work your way through the WIFM system. At this point, we want to avoid describing the customer because to position a brand correctly using the WIFM philosophy of marketing requires the marketer to position the brand at needs first and people last. This is likely to be a foreign concept for marketers because we have been taught to think precisely the other way around—to describe the target group first, then think of their needs.

The Mistake of Selecting a Target Group First

When you were taught to describe the target group first, it seemed to make good sense; you never questioned it. After all, the message has to be aimed at someone to be cost-efficient, and the media department of the agency has to buy ads that will appeal to a certain demographic segment. You also have to distribute your product in a location that is convenient for the target market to buy it. These are real considerations, and important ones to boot. But they are important only *after* the brand positioning has been set.

When we are looking at needs, the obvious question is, Whose needs? I guess that's why most marketing texts suggest specifying the target group first and then the target message. But the more I've worked at brand-positioning, the more I've come to realize that marketers can severely damage their brands by specifying the target group first.

Disaster 1: Specifying the Wrong Target Group

One of the major problems with specifying the target group before specifying the needs being met is that you might specify the wrong target group. This is especially serious when you are developing new brands and there are very few knowns. The result is that your needs search will be among the wrong group of potential customers.

I once had the privilege of developing a higher-priced beer, John Labatt Classic, which is the super-premium beer of Canada. At the outset of the project, we recruited respondents for our market research who were upscale and affluent to tell us what they wanted in a beer that would make it of higher value to them. As we had been trained, we made an assumption about the target group first and then tried to find our WIFM among this group. We got very strange answers from these people. Most did not even want what we had to offer. Then it dawned on us that we were assuming that you had to be upscale and affluent to want a higher-quality, higher-priced beer. We then turned the question around and recruited respondents who believed that:

- Not all beers taste the same.
- A domestic brewery could make a superior beer.
- It was worthwhile to pay a premium for something superior.

We obtained these characteristics from the original research that suggested an opportunity for the brand in the first place.

Only then did the whole project come together. Instead of making a predetermined judgment about whom the brand would appeal to, we recruited respondents on the basis of needs that a super-premium beer was likely to fulfill. The people we were now talking to came from all walks of life. Some were teachers, some were carpenters, and some (but not many) were executives. They had nothing in common socioeconomically or demographically, and they were certainly quite different from one another in life-styles and personalities. They had, however, the one commonality that the brand was built on: They all wanted the best beer a domestic brewer could make. Some in this target group were relatively poor, and some were relatively rich. But it didn't matter because the product category is inexpensive. Socioeconomics doesn't enter into the decision to indulge oneself with the best beer available.

When we eventually put the message (our WIFM) ahead of the target group in our brand positioning, it became clear that the need we were developing the brand for had nothing to do with a predefined demographic group. If we had continued to develop the brand for upscale portions of the market, as we originally set out to do, we probably would have put off the more downscale portions of the market and dampened sales. Since the upscale portions of the market had no need for what John Labatt Classic had to offer, testing our liquid or packaging or advertising among this incorrect target market would have steered us in the wrong direction. This misdirection would, in turn, have steered the brand away from meeting the needs of the group that had a legitimate need for what John Labatt Classic had to offer. In a nutshell, had we targeted John Labatt Classic at the upscale portions of the market, the brand would likely have failed.

What I learned from this example is that needs are much greater and more homogeneous than people.

Disaster 2: Narrowing the Target Group

Almost as bad as picking the wrong target group is targeting at one demographic or personality group to the exclusion of others. Positioning a brand in this way is absolutely forbidden in WIFM marketing because there is a pretty high probability that you will sell a lot less of your brand than you would like to.

The reason for this is that you are narrowing the target group before accounting for acceptance or rejection of the brand based on its ability to satisfy specific needs better than other brands. So if you decide right away that you are going to target the brand only at working women, for example, you may offend nonworking women who might be equally accepting of your brand because it performs a task better than every other brand in the category. You will wind up with a much smaller absolute volume than if you started with no preconceived notions about the target group at all. Our OMNIPOTENT 1 example from Chapter 2 did this by initially limiting the target market to teens, when the underlying human need for freedom from domination cuts across a much wider demographic spectrum. Johnson's Baby Shampoo increased its volume exponentially after taking off the target group blinders and realizing that the need for gentleness in a shampoo isn't limited to babies.

A headline in the April 11, 1988, issue of *Marketing* magazine reads: ROCK BAND TO BEAT THE DRUM FOR [a major brand of breath fresheners]. The body copy goes on to say, "The combined advertising/promotion event is part of a move by [the brand] to target teens and young adults to the brand."

Now I don't know why the marketers of this well-known brand of breath freshener decided to do this, but my guess is that the decision had nothing to do with the needs the brand fulfills in the marketplace. I can tell you from personal experience that this brand fulfills my need for fresh breath very well, and for me, it does so better than any other breath freshener out there. For me, the brand's WIFM is: It freshens breath better than every other brand in the product class. Yet I am no longer in the target group, according to this article.

This targeting likely resulted in a number of older users leaving the brand. When older users suddenly saw teens being targeted in the advertising, they probably began to question whether the product had been reformulated to appeal more to teenage tastes. Since only about 10 percent of the population is made up of teens, why would a marketer exclude the other 90 percent?

Perhaps the marketer honestly, but erroneously, believed that there were no real differences between brands, so he thought he had to create meaningful differences based on users. Perhaps, like me, he was trained to designate a target group first and then devise a message that would appeal to the target. Perhaps the marketer was afraid to try something different from the tried and true formula that has been used in marketing for years. Perhaps teens had a low per capita usage of the brand and he was trying to increase it. Or perhaps the marketer thought it was too difficult to vary the product to meet people's needs, so instead, he varied the target group to match the brand. Perhaps he was afraid that if he didn't target, he would be accused of trying to be all things to all people, which he knew from experience he could not be. Most likely, however, like us when we first started to work on John Labatt Classic, he never thought about the implications of a target group and just automatically selected one because that's what marketers are supposed to do.

We have been trained to think that it makes sense to specify the target group first. After all, isn't it logical, in the breath freshener example, that the needs of teenagers must be different from the needs of their parents? So if I zero in on the needs of teenagers, I can design brands that are better suited to their needs. Sounds logical doesn't it?

The problem is that marketers who think this way make a terrible mistake—they mix the general with the specific. Of course the needs of teenagers are different from the needs of their parents, but *only in a general sense*, not necessarily when it comes to things like breath fresheners. There are potential consumers with similar breath-freshening needs in both the teen and the parent demographic categories. In terms of the need for a breath freshener, the differences between teens and parents do not exist.

Certain groups tend to become popular targets of marketers. Yuppies, for example, were a favorite target in the 1980s. Now the aging baby boomers—the "grey market"—are the focus. A *Marketing* magazine article (January 16, 1989) mentions that "more than half of this country's discretionary income" comes from consumers over 50 years of age.

Although it seems to make sense for marketers to channel their efforts where the money is, the presumption is that the needs of people over 50, *in a general sense*, are different from the needs of people under 50. This may be true for a few product classes, but for the bulk of consumer products, services, and brands, the age or socioeconomic status of consumers has nothing to do with their need for brands. For example, older people with their own teeth have just as strong a need for toothpaste as younger people with their own teeth. Too many marketers are chasing the grey market these days, whether the "greys" have specific needs that their brands fulfill or not.

Another problem of targeting people rather than needs is that when marketers target a particular group, they group members as part of a homogeneous whole, without recognizing the diversity and individuality of members, or the different subgroups that make up the segment. Let me show you what happens when marketers try to target a brand at a specific target group rather than at a specific consumer need. Suppose the marketers of the breath freshener had said: "Okay, we'll buy this idea of WIFMs, but let's confine our investigation of WIFMs to teens, because we honestly believe that we can do a better job in meeting needs if we zero in on a more specific group at the outset. Perhaps teens have a specific need to hide cigarette or alcohol odors that is different from the needs of older adults. We won't know this unless we isolate this group."

So they go down to the local high school to study teen needs. The first thing they notice is a teen with spiked orange hair wearing an expensive, studded, black leather jacket. Then they notice several other teens wearing Esprit sweatshirts. Then they notice a bunch of guys walking down the hall all wearing the same team sports jackets.

They are directed by the principal to talk to the Student Council for assistance. They are relieved to note that most of the Student Council members look "normal" in their polo shirts and jeans. They feel an empathy with this group and tell them so. There is a long discussion about the different groups of teens at the high school, and one of the marketers notes that hairstyle and dress code pretty much distinguish the various groups. She has seen, right before her eyes, a real-life example of life-style segmentation, and the various groups will make a great series of commercials, with an almost endless pool of possibilities.

Then someone pours cold water on the whole thing by asking, "But what has life-style got to do with a teenager's need for a particular brand of breath freshener?" There is a long silence as everyone tries to think up a logical reason why a teen with a green mohawk would need a breath freshener more than a teen in a polo shirt, or vice versa. One person argues that the teen with the green mohawk needs a breath freshener because he probably drinks and smokes to show the world how independent he is. Some agree. Others challenge this statement. They say, "The kids in the polo shirts need breath fresheners more because they are one of the few groups that can afford to buy liquor at today's prices. And anyway, the polo shirt group is the 'in' crowd, so it's more important for them to be appealing to the opposite sex." Then someone argues from another perspective.

They all argue their various positions until they realize that there are many teen groups with a legitimate need to freshen their breath, just as there are a host of adult groups with the same need. Finally the realization that they are addressing the consumers' need for the product class rather than the need for their specific brand leads them back to the drawing board.

When they finally do market research among teens and their parents, they find that there is a need to freshen breath among certain teens and among certain parents regardless of hairstyle or socioeconomic status. They also learn that groupings of people may or may not have anything to do with their need for a product class or brand. Just because we can easily identify teenagers as a group doesn't mean that they are all alike and will all respond to brands or product classes in a similar manner. They are intelligent and individualized consumers. WIFMs recognize this individuality by specifying the needs to be met first.

Disaster 3: Missing an Important WIFM

We see the most common example of missing important WIFMs on our television screens every day. This is what is commonly referred to as life-style brand positioning, in which the marketer does a generalized life-style or psychographic study that categorizes consumers based on their motivations for buying things.

Usually the life-style segments are given names like "Innovators" or "Achievers," and the names usually relate to what drives (motivates) them to buy things generally. The theory goes that the Innovator is driven by a need to buy brands that are new and different, and the Achiever is more quality or image oriented.

The life-style positioner then links the brand under scrutiny to a life-style segment through one of two methods. The first method is to use the generalized life-cycle theory, which holds that in many product categories the Innovator is the first to adopt new brands. Therefore, if yours is a new brand it should be targeted at Innovators, and the brand positioning should tap into the Innovators' need to innovate.

The second and most common way to life-style position is to look at the seeming benefit of a brand and try to tie it back to the generalized need of the life-style segment. For example, a high-quality brand would be targeted at Achievers, who have a need for brands with high-quality images.

In both instances, the life-style positioner is making too many leaps too early and likely missing some important needs that the brand could fulfill better than the competition. Worse still, both life-style positioning theories start with generalities to prove the specific, and both generalities may be wrong.

Although it is true that Innovators innovate, they most often innovate in the first entry in a new product class, not the second or third entry. So even though your brand may be new to you, it may not be new in the Innovators' vocabulary if it is the second or later brand in the product category. To them it may seem like a clone of an existing brand, not something new. Are they likely to switch to it? No, because it doesn't meet their need to innovate. We should be searching for another of the Innovators' needs to tie the brand to when we hunt for a WIFM.

Life-style positioners make even bigger mistakes when they attempt to position a seeming benefit of the brand to the seeming need of a life-style segment. Once again the mistakes can be traced to the use of generalities to arrive at a specific conclusion. First, the life-style positioner assumes that all Achievers buy *every product class*. But there probably aren't too many Achievers who buy the highest-quality steel-toed work boots, so the assumption is flawed. What we have seen in every life-style study we've undertaken is that Achievers *tend* to buy the highest quality of every product class they enter, but they make lots of exceptions to this general rule, depending on the brand offerings. For example, the highest quality beef in the world is supposed to be Kobe beef from Japan. Over a two-year period, Japanese cattle are fed grain marinated in beer. Then, toward the end of their lives, the cattle are hand-massaged to break up the fat. The result is the beautiful marbled look that is prized by the connoisseurs of Shabu-shabu. Unfortunately, Kobe beef sells for $135 a pound in the United States, and few Achievers can afford to buy it.

What you will find after following the WIFM system completely and in sequence is that positioning a brand at people, whether they are described demographically, emotionally, or psychographically, is in most cases incorrect.

Determining the Message First

The WIFM system demands that when formulating a brand's position, you sort out the WIFM message first. The group of people whose needs are fulfilled by your WIFM message is then the target market.

Sometimes the target defined by need fulfillment matches a demographic characteristic. When this happens, the targeting job is easy. In most cases, however, the target will cut across a wide swath of demography and geography. This may seem problematic when it comes to media buying or distribution, but unless you promote and distribute widely, you will be limiting the potential sale of your brand. The problem is only as large as your ability to finance the promotion or distribution, which can be handled through good cost-benefit analysis.

The first place to start looking for needs in an established product category is by identifying everyone who now uses the product category or categories like it. Make this user group as broad as possible at this stage, because you don't want to exclude anyone who might be important in determining the brand's position. With new products you may have to be a little more creative, as with the John Labatt Classic example earlier.

You can make assumptions based on needs that are being fulfilled by other, similar product classes to ascertain the potential target group for a new product. Often just thinking about where a new product would fit in Maslow's hierarchy (see Chapter 2) provides the necessary clues. To specify the target group based on demographics, life-styles, or personalities, however, virtually guarantees an incorrect brand position or, worse still, no position at all.

Recently I was involved in new product development for a completely new brand that, if successful, would carve out a new subsegment of an existing product class and, in so doing, likely steal some business from some contiguous product categories. To avoid the mistake of narrowing the target group too early, we designed our market research to be as broadly based as possible. We included a small sample of every type of person that the project team thought could be a potential consumer of the brand (whose needs were fulfilled by the brand). This made the research a little more expensive, but we controlled the expense by obtaining minimum sample sizes in each cell of potential users. The cost was cheap compared to the potential lost revenue from narrowing the target group right off the bat. We then let the respondents in our market research tell us whether they were interested in the brand through well-executed product/concept testing. As expected, some groups were interested and others weren't. But when we were finished, we knew exactly whom the brand would appeal to as well as the specific product classes and brands the new product would hurt.

Corporate Needs vs. Consumer Needs

Perhaps worse than targeting at people rather than needs is the manufacturer that does its needs homework, identifies the needs that have to be met, and then ties the hands of the marketing group by imposing financial or other corporate criteria that make needs fulfillment next to impossible. In other words, company needs get in the way of fulfilling consumer needs.

The two most common examples of this I call the "Cannibalization Factor" and "Following the Followers."

The Cannibalization Factor

Suppose you, the marketer, do your needs homework and find that about one quarter of the current consumers of your product class have a need for a radically different version of the product. They are buying the current product, but they are not happy with any of the brands in the product class, including yours. Solid, quantitatively based market research has shown that if you change your current product to meet their needs better, you will steal some market share from competitive brands and cement the loyalty of existing customers. You therefore decide to subsegment the market to offer two versions of your existing brand: the current version and a modified version to meet the needs of the group that are unhappy with the current version. Today's the big day. You stand up in front of the management group to get the approval to proceed and, with a dazzling set of overhead projector slides, you take them through the logic of adding a new offering to the line. The statistics are unassailable—or so you think. The new subsegment will garner market share points resulting in profits of $20 million a year once the brand is established in the marketplace. All the company has to do is make a substantial up-front investment, and the payout will come two years down the road.

You sit down in triumph after showing company management how long-term profitability can be improved and await its approval. Then the bomb falls out of the lips of the financial guru of the company: "Did you take into account, in your financial projections, the fact that you will be cannibalizing current users of the brand to a great extent with your new brand?"

You are caught with your pants down because you don't even understand what *cannibalization* means in the business world. What the financial wizard is saying is that since many of the customers for the new brand will come from existing brands, you should discount your financial projections and take into account the financial contribution of only additional users—either new users to the category or competitive users that have been stolen. He then does a quick recalculation based on new users and states that it will take twice as long to reach the payout you projected—and a four-year payout is outside the company's financial policy of three-year paybacks. Your project is in jeopardy, and you know it. You reach for straws, but to no avail: "Our market research shows that these customers are not happy with current offerings in the product class. That suggests that they are likely to leave the product class unless one of the companies delivers what they want. So why should we calculate the profit on only additional users the new brand will attract?" But since you can't say how many current users will leave the category (the truth is that until someone gives them an alternative, many of them will stick to existing brands), your project goes down in flames.

What has happened here is a perfect illustration of how a cautious management group can destroy an attempt to deliver to consumers what they want and need. What the accountant did was ignore the fact that a smart competitor could easily do the same thing—subsegment the market and deliver a brand that better met consumers' needs. The brand manager should have asked the accountant about opportunity losses: "How would you calculate the company's profit if XYZ introduces the new subsegment before we do and we lose three points of market share?" That may not win the argument if the company is extremely cautious, but it at least puts the Cannibalization Factor into a more realistic context—a context that puts customer needs ahead of short-term financial needs.

Following the Followers

The second major way to scuttle a perfectly good needs-fulfillment opportunity is to take the "Chicken Approach" to brand positioning, which relies on targeting at people rather than needs. Suppose a certain brand of motorcycle has reached the peak of its life cycle and is starting to decline. What would the motorcycle marketer do? In all likelihood he would start by defining the needs of consumers. Then he would try to get permission from management to make a change in the brand offering in order to better meet certain consumer needs. If his suggestion is too radical (in the eyes of management), in all likelihood the request will be denied. The first question management asks is, "What effect will the proposed change have on current users of the brand?" If there is any possible negative effect at all, the proposal will be turned down flat by a company-driven management style that is afraid to take chances. The motorcycle marketer is driven back to narrowing his needs search to current users of the brand because of the roadblock set up by management. He refines the brand slightly so that it better meets the needs of current users only.

Such an approach to marketing is more the norm than the exception in North American marketing today. Brands change slowly over time because marketers are continually looking at the needs of current users and excluding the needs of nonusers. Such an approach may make short-term financial sense for the company, but in the long run, this strategy leaves huge holes in the marketplace that a smart competitor can leverage to its advantage. For example, the Japanese revolutionized the motor-cycle market. While North American marketers of motorcycles were focused on the Hell's Angels types, who were pretty happy with their big Harley-Davidsons, the Japanese were uncovering the need for smaller, lighter, more versatile bikes.

The Chicken Approach to brand modification focuses solely on current users and measures their wants and needs at various points in time. But, for well-established brands, current users are essentially "followers," not "brand leaders." They are happy with the status quo because they are happy being followers; they generally don't like change. Marketers can always find some small thing to change to make the brand better for current users, but in so doing, they have sown the seeds of a brand's inevitable death, because they are following the followers, not the brand leaders. This is the "don't fix it if it ain't broke" brand-positioning approach, but for brand leaders, the brand is already "broke."

Most brands require radical treatment every so often to keep them in tune with the needs of brand leaders. This is more revolutionary than evolutionary, and it requires a willingness to take risks. Time will tell, but my guess is that marketers can no longer afford to be evolutionary when they are hard-pressed by strong competitors. More importantly, marketers can no longer afford to be evolutionary when they are hard-pressed by con-sumers to fulfill their needs.

No matter how it's done, brands must keep up with the wants and needs of the category leaders rather than just taking into account current users' needs, or the brand will die. Marketers and their managements have to stop targeting at people rather than needs. These cautious corporate philosophies tie the marketers' hands and give strong, hungry competitors the opportunity to either follow brand leaders or cannibalize brands and chip away at the outside of every market, until there is no center left in any market.

5

Considering All Needs

To arrive at a solid brand strategy that will bind consumers to your brand forever, you must look at *all* the potential needs at the start of the brand-positioning process. Don't be tempted to forgo the examination of all the needs at this stage. To do so can be fatal to a brand.

There are five people needs and fourteen brand value needs (listed below).

People Needs	Brand Value Needs
1. Human	1. Sensory/performance
2. Socio-geo-demographic	2. Quality
3. Occasions-for-use	3. Durability
4. Emotional	4. Ease of use
5. Life-style	5. Packaging
	6. Pricing
	7. Availability
	8. Variety of choice
	9. Service
	10. Healthfulness
	11. Environmental friendliness
	12. Popularity
	13. Promotions
	14. Advertising

People Needs

I call the following needs *people needs* because they are essentially just different ways to describe people outwardly, inwardly, and the way they behave as people.

Human Needs

First, consumers have the fundamental human needs that Maslow categorized for us in the 1940s (see Chapter 2). These needs arise just because the consumer is a live, functioning human being who thinks and feels. Heredity and environment play a role in structuring human needs, and the needs for many brands can be accurately pinpointed on one of the five levels of Maslow's hierarchy. For example, esteem needs were used quite successfully by Babe perfume and Virginia Slims cigarettes in creating unique niches for themselves in the marketplace. They have also been at the root of much of today's human-rights movement.

Socio-Geo-Demographic Needs

Next there are demographic, geographic, and socioeconomic characteristics that, when layered onto the underlying human needs, create subsegments of a category. These needs can be advantageous for some product categories and catastrophic for others. The classic example of where geography works against you is trying to sell refrigerators to Inuits or furnaces to Caribbeans.

Occasion-for-Use Needs

Various needs arise because an individual puts or finds himself in a certain situation. These are called occasion-for-use needs and, from my observations, this seems to be a favorite way to position brands.

The occasion-for-use strategy stresses the need to use one brand in one situation and another brand, of the same product class, in another situation. The reason for different brands is that each situation is so fundamentally different that the product has to be changed slightly to better meet the needs of that situation.

No one brand can meet all the conditions imposed by all occasions. For example, think about the different needs that are satisfied by two beverages—one after you've just run a marathon, and another after you've just come in from skiing and settled down in front of the fire with your fiancée.

Automobiles are another obvious example when it comes to the different needs that have to be met under different circumstances. Four-wheel-drive automobiles are better than two-wheel-drive when driving in a severe snowstorm. This type of scenario has been used quite effectively by Subaru.

Not so obvious are other product categories such as computers. Compaque carved out quite a niche for itself by delivering high-quality portability to the computer market. In fact, some predict that lap-top computers will replace personal computers in the office and home in the very near future. You have to take your hat off to Compaque for understanding that a good WIFM can be delivered when a brand can be tailor-made to appeal to occasion-for-use needs. The Amstrad ad pictured exploits the occasion-for-use theme well in its visual.

Emotional Needs

Another type of need arises from the emotional state people find themselves in under certain circumstances. For example, wouldn't your beverage choice change if you came in from skiing, settled down in front of the fireplace with your fiancée—and were told that she was about to run off to Switzerland with the ski instructor? You would be in a foul mood, and your need for something to calm yourself or forget your problems would not likely be satisfied with hot cocoa.

Many refer to emotional needs as moods, but I find this definition too limiting because it suggests something transitory. Emotions can be temporary or permanent. They can be deep-seated feelings that arise as a result of a strongly held attitude, such as those of an animal-rights supporter. Or they can be transitory emotional states, such as someone who had a bad day at the office.

The ad for Sunlight dishwashing detergent illustrates the

use of emotions in advertising. And Sunlight uses the magic WIFM word *nothing* in its ad: NOTHING GETS GLASSES MORE SPOTLESS! So there, Mr. and Mrs. Consumer, is the reason Sunlight is superior to every other dishwashing detergent.

Not so obvious is the emotion that is created by the product category itself: the whole area of attitudes or beliefs that are held about the category in question. Take cigarettes, for example. For some, the mere mention of cigarettes is a red flag that produces instant anger. For them, cigarettes do not meet any need. They cannot figure out how in the world cigarettes can possibly fulfill a need for anyone unless they have a "death wish." The cigarette industry has learned that nonsmokers' emotions and the needs resulting from these emotions have to be taken into account, just as the needs of smokers have to be catered to. When the industry ignored the needs of nonsmokers, it was legislated into taking them into account. Witness the warning labels on cigarette packages and the segregation in restaurants and airplanes based on smoking preference. Witness the recent legislation in several cities that effectively bans smoking in offices.

Life-Style Needs

Finally, we have the needs that arise because of the consumer's life-style. Much of the work in this area has been driven by life-style or psychographic market research, in which the marketer asks consumers to rate themselves on a battery of scales that reveal their attitudes, feelings, thoughts, and reactions to life in general. Respondents are then grouped into homogeneous clusters of individuals with similar outlooks on life. The groups are given names like "Achievers" or "Innovators" or "Conservatives" to indicate the underlying human motivations for buying things. The "New Values" consumer of the 1990s was first spotted through life-style research. During the 1980s, consumers almost burned themselves out trying to keep up with the glitz and status symbols. But the former "shop till you drop" consumer has now opted for a simpler life full of things that really matter: family, friends, recreation, and spirituality.

Brand Value Needs

In addition to the needs of people themselves, there is another set of variables that brands bring to the purchase decision, just because of the way they look or how they perform a certain task. These value-added variables are those areas manufacturers can change to better meet the needs of consumers. And because they are variable, they can add extra value to the brand over and above the fulfillment of the general people needs outlined above. (See Chapter 8 for more on brand values.)

Automobiles from Japan, for example, hit the North American market like a storm in the late 1960s, because they met real consumer needs that the North American automakers hadn't been paying attention to. In fact, the differences were so obvious that you could see and feel the benefits of Japanese cars over North American cars. Japanese cars were, to many consumers, excellent examples of how a combination of sensory/performance superiority, quality of manufacturing (such as fit and finish), product durability, ease of use (and fun to use), packaging, and fair pricing can beat out competition that has lost sight of consumer needs. These brand values won a massive market share against marketers who emphasized people-type WIFMs.

When an industry is very competitive, the emphasis should be on the value-added characteristics of brands—things such as superior design, taste, smell, feel, sound of a brand; superior performance; functionality of packaging; quality of fit and finish; durability; ease of use; price; promotional elements; range of choice; popularity; after-sales service; advertising; how healthy and environmentally friendly a brand is; and, last but not least, how easy the brand is to find and buy.

Interaction of All Needs

The different types of consumer needs are interrelated when it comes to brand selection. The intelligent WIFM marketer looks at the interrelationship among *all* the needs—the five people needs as well as the fourteen brand value needs—to find a superiority claim on which to base a brand's position in the marketplace.

I cannot say this strongly enough: *Do not bypass any of the nineteen need types when you are trying to determine your brand's position.* During the past two decades, marketers have repeatedly made this mistake, and in my judgement, this is the primary reason so much customer loyalty has been lost.

Many brand positioners have focused exclusively on the five people needs and have become obsessed with consumer psychology. This shaky basis for brand positioning has led to the wholesale destruction of formerly strong brand images and is the primary reason that many marketers have turned their backs on advertising's ability to move products and have instead spent so much money on push tactics such as promotions. This single-minded focus on consumer psychology by advertisers is one of the primary reasons consumers are zapping so many commercials these days.

Chasing the Wrong Strategy

For as long as I can remember, the TV audience measurement services have been trying to use life-styles to discriminate between viewers of different types of programs. And for as long as I can remember, they have failed.

One audience measurement service assumed that the reason that its data showed that Yuppies tended to watch the same types of shows as "Conservatives" was because life-styles were not being measured correctly. So it hired two of the best research houses that specialize in life-style/psychographic research. After two attempts and several hundreds of thousands of dollars, they came up empty again. According to a report in the October 16, 1989, issue of *Marketing:* "The discrimination between program types and the [life-style] segments is not wide."

After spending so much time and effort trying to prove that a people-type theory of brand positioning applies to media strategy, the service concluded in the *Marketing* article that the reason for the lack of discrimination "may be a function of the medium itself as a mass vehicle or the ubiquitous appeal of the shows themselves." This reason alone should have suggested that it was not looking at needs in the correct way. Yet after all this effort and expense, and after proving conclusively that measuring people types does not predict their viewing preferences, this audience measurement service is going to spend an enormous amount of money in another attempt to make it work. Almost three decades and hundreds of attempts at trying to use life-styles to distinguish between program viewing should have proved to everyone by now that life-style is the wrong needs area.

I have concluded that there are two major reasons that television viewing does not tie directly to the life-styles of viewers. It is clear that the primary consumer need that television meets is entertainment. To assume that Yuppies are entertained differently from Conservatives is a false assumption based on a prediction from the general to the specific. Just because Yuppies need quality in the products and brands they buy (the general) doesn't mean that quality motivates them to watch one type of program over another (the specific). Quality may have nothing to do with the types of programs that provide entertainment to an individual. For example, I can be extremely quality conscious and still be entertained by a suspense program or a sitcom as much as by a documentary. To me TV is a passive entertainment vehicle that I use to fulfill my need for relaxation, which can be satisfied by a wide variety of program types. What's that got to do with the fact the Yuppie is an Achiever? Absolutely nothing! Quality is a totally different motivation that just doesn't apply in this situation.

The other reason that life-style groupings don't relate to program types is that TV broadcasters put shows on the air that will attract the largest audiences. That's what mass-appeal broadcasting is all about—reaching the greatest number of people in a single program so the broadcasters can meet the cost-per-thousand needs of advertisers. It makes good economic sense for broadcasters to think this way. To then assume that a specific life-style segment would be entertained by different programs, when the majority of programs are not designed to be narrowly targeted, makes the life-style proposition illogical.

Derived Benefits

There is a new theory of positioning called *derived benefits* that, on the surface, seems to make a lot of sense. What this positioning theory suggests is that an advertiser should not list any of the fourteen brand values in an ad because the poor consumer will become too bogged down in detail. Instead, the advertiser should promote what all this information means to the consumer— the Derived Benefit. In other words, promote the "bottom line."

As an example, Downy fabric softener has built its number-one market-share position by promoting a lot of details such as softness, no static cling, and an "April-fresh" smell. However, the brand strategist is concerned that the amount of detail the consumer has to remember about Downy might be overwhelming—a legitimate concern. Instead of all this detail, the advertiser is told to use the Derived Benefit, DOWNY GIVES CLOTHES A NO-TICEABLE IMPROVEMENT, on the assumption that this bottom-line statement communicates to users that their families will appreciate the extra effort they make to soften clothes.

It should be noted that the Derived Benefits theory shouldn't be used by relatively new brands. Instead, new brands *should* give consumers details, because it may be difficult to convince consumers of a Derived Benefit until the advertiser has had the time to convince them that the brand can deliver on its claim.

The Downy example plus this latter caution suggests to me that the Derived Benefit brand-positioning technique is just another example of not taking into account other important needs when determining a brand's strategy. It could lead the marketer into a needs area that is totally inappropriate for the brand. In fact, I think Downy would lose a lot of its market share if it followed this strategist's advice. My concern for Downy would be that if the brand manager used Derived Benefits in positioning the brand, he would leave a huge hole in the brand's flank for a smart competitor to drive a tank through. My guess is that if the Downy brand manager looked at the brand's penetration by life-style segment, he would find that Downy had high penetration among consumers who need to be appreciated by their families. But Downy probably also has high penetration in most other life-style segments within the fabric softener category

—market leaders often do. And that's the problem with this and all brand positionings that ignore other important needs: Zeroing in on only one generalized people need narrows the target group prematurely and leaves a huge opportunity for a smart competitor. If Downy walks away from its position as the leading brand with the freshest smell that softens and leaves no static cling and starts to talk in generalized terms about the needs of the one life-style segment containing people who wish to be appreciated by family members, competitors have many more positioning options at their disposal. They can, for example, beef up their brand offerings in certain product-related areas and start to make claims about their superiority in softening, static cling, or fresh smell, since Downy no longer says these things. Or the competitor can address another life-style segment— perhaps the less self-conscious, pragmatic person who just doesn't like to lie on hard, wrinkled sheets at night. What happens to brand loyalty if this happens? It's lower, to be sure.

Needs are much greater and much more homogeneous than people. To position Downy on anything less than the brand values it fulfills does a disservice to this excellent brand.

The general premise behind the Derived Benefits positioning theory is that consumers don't like to get bogged down with details. I think that's true. But why would the marketing strategist then assume that this generality should lead the marketer of Downy to look for a need in another needs area? Perhaps the Derived Benefits strategist is correct; perhaps three needs is too much information for the consumer to assimilate. But that doesn't mean that Downy should walk away from all three needs it fulfills. Perhaps its best position would be to focus on the biggest of these three needs and abandon the other two. That would be a better position for the brand than abandoning the needs that made it such a huge success in the first place.

Much learning has taken place in the area of applying people needs to business since the father of motivational research, Ernest Dichter, first showed business how to apply consumer psychology to marketing in the early 1940s. But we need to learn a lot more. To narrow a needs search to just one needs area to the exclusion of other needs, or to zero in on people needs and ignore the fourteen brand value needs, may be the largest single mistake a brand strategist can make. To do the positioning job correctly, you must look at all the potential needs for the product class and brand. Only then can the sorting process take place in an orderly fashion.

6

Brands vs.
Product Classes

In any brand-positioning exercise, marketers are attempting to answer one question: Why would someone select my brand over someone else's brand? But what is a brand anyway? Does it really matter whether we talk about a product class or a brand?

By *brand*, I mean a specific variant of the product class that bears a proprietary or, in most cases, a trademarked name, such as IBM or BMW. By *product class*, I mean the name of the business classification that one is engaged in, such as computers or automobiles. All the brands together constitute the product class.

Product classes can have subsegments. For example, station wagons are a subsegment of the main product class of automobiles. This is essentially what market segmentation is all about, chopping up the main product class into smaller segments that meet unique and more finely targeted needs.

Brands evolved because consumers had certain fundamental needs that no single variant of the product class could meet alone. The brands themselves brought new variables to the equation that went beyond pure product class needs. For example, when my grandmother was a girl, people used baking soda to clean their teeth. Then a brand marketer came up with flavored tooth powder that offered the benefit of pleasant taste to the teeth-cleaning experience. Then another brand marketer turned the powder into paste. Anyone who has ever used tooth powder will tell you that you got as much powder in the sink as you did on the toothbrush. Toothpastes overcame this problem and offered the consumer a real benefit of convenient usage. But more importantly, toothpaste offered consumers an additional choice in the marketplace. Then came real market segmentation based on subdividing the market into smaller and smaller needs groupings: toothpaste that prevents cavities; different flavors of toothpaste; toothpaste in the form of a gel; toothpaste with mouthwash in it; toothpaste in a pump dispenser; toothpaste that reduces plaque; and today's latest innovation—toothpaste that comes in a stand-up tube that is more environmentally friendly because it eliminates the need for excess packaging. Clearly, one brand could not handle all the innovation in this market over the past twenty-five years, so market segmentation with real brand differentiation took place. But within the staggering number of segments and subsegments in every product category, there are usually three to five brands slugging it out for dominant market-share position. It's a war, and the brand that meets the consumers' needs better within a market segment will win it. In other words, the war is all about superiority.

The Competition

If one brand could meet all the needs of the product class, the brand would be the product class. If the OMNIPOTENT 1 were the only 1960s-styled sports car, we could have sold it on its product class merits because the brand and the product class would be one. But once there is competition, it isn't enough to tell consumers that your brand meets the needs of the product class or subproduct class without tying the benefits of the brand to the specific needs that your brand meets better than other brands in the category.

Suppose a vacuum cleaner salesman came to your door with a one-line pitch that is supposed to persuade you to buy: His vacuum cleaner sucks up dust. That's all he tells you—it sucks up dust. Would you buy his vacuum cleaner? Not a chance! Every vacuum sucks up dust. He hasn't given you a reason to buy. Yet hundreds of millions of dollars are spent every year by beverage manufacturers to tell you that their beverages are refreshing. And another few hundred million dollars are spent by hotels telling you that their hotels are comfortable. So what! These statements are no different from the salesman telling you that the vacuum sucks up dust. However, the beverage manufacturer that can tell you why its beverage is more refreshing than every other beverage on the market would have a strong WIFM. So would the hotel that could truly demonstrate that it was more comfortable than all the rest. So would the vacuum cleaner salesman who could demonstrate that his vacuum cleaner sucked up dust better than every other machine on the market.

Knowing the difference between product classes and brands is the key to brand positioning. It is the principal ingredient in arriving at a WIFM brand position based on superiority.

The background of how I arrived at brand versus product class differentiation as the primary ingredient in WIFM brand positioning is presented next in the hope that those who are currently using consumer psychology as the basic platform for their brand positions will rethink their focus.

The Badge Theory

Back in the early 1970s, when marketers first started to experiment with identifying people needs, most of our work was based on the hypothesis that brands had personalities. My colleagues and I adopted a routine in almost all focus groups to capture the essence of the personality of each of the brands we were working on. We said to consumers, "Pretend this brand is a person; describe her; tell us what she looks like; how old she is; what kind of a house she lives in." Personalities emerged for all our brands and for the competitors' too.

It was fun to do research that way, and we were very excited about the results, as were the advertising agencies. They had been saying for several years that the consumer wears a brand like a badge of distinction—as an extension of his or her own personality. You can get an idea of what is meant by "an extension of the personality" by examining the ad for Quorum, a

QUORUM

Introducing Quorum. A fragrance for the other man lurking inside you.

After Shave
After Shave Balm
Eau de toilette
Eau de toilette Spray
Deodorant Stick
Individual Soap

men's cologne. Quorum appears to be a not-too-subtle badge for a man to wear that communicates, "The devil made me do it."

I call this way of thinking Badge Theory. (Others erroneously call it Brand Personality Theory, and I explain the difference in Chapter 12.)

Humanizing Brands

The minute the advertising agencies talked about consumers wearing our brands like badges, we bred more personality into our brands. Our ads focused less on the features of our brands that made them superior to the competition (WIFMs) and more on the soft sell—occasion-for-use, emotional, and personality factors. These measures of consumer psychology became our Unique Selling Propositions (USPs). We discussed for hours the mood of each commercial, the setting, the tone, and especially the casting. If consumers wore our brands as an expression of their personalities, then we had to carefully deliver the right personality message (image) in such a way that consumers would be proud to wear our badge. The words *empathy* and *emotion* started to take over advertising discussions. We even developed an advertising testing procedure that measured emotional responses to advertising. It also measured the main message, as our previous market research had done, but since we didn't really have a main message anymore, the focus of attention was on the soft-sell, emotional responses.

Like a human being, each of our brands was perceived as a living, breathing, feeling, emotive, responsive individual, and our measurements of the health of this individual became clinical in many ways. Rather than asking consumers if the brand delivered the brand values to their satisfaction (our old measure of the main message of the commercial), we started to look hard at the physical and mental health of the brand. We measured our brand's heart rate (Is the ad exciting?), we took its temperature (Is the ad boring?), and we analyzed the ad's psyche in various ways (Is the ad irritating, likable, fun, unusual? Is the enthusiasm of the ad catching?). Ads were regularly discarded not because they weren't delivering a message, but because the advertising wasn't meeting someone's emotional needs. The reason for advertising changed from persuading potential customers to buy a brand because it met their needs, to doing something that consumers could empathize with based on their deep-seated psychological needs.

Overnight, production costs for a single advertisement doubled. The advertising agency justified the additional cost by arguing that given our new way of thinking, it was necessary to get the right production values into the commercials—the right mood, the perfect setting, and characters that consumers would empathize with. Commercials were shot in exotic locations such as the Caribbean, Hawaii, and Australia, and every brand manager aspired to work in the advertising department because the perquisites were fantastic.

Categorizing Consumers

The bulk of the Badge Theory work carried out by my colleagues and me revolved around a huge life-style study among users of our product class. We conducted this research on the premise that if consumers were wearing our brands like a badge, we had better line up the right brands with the right groups of consumers. Our goal was to categorize users of our product class by people types based on attitudes toward life and behavior in general.

We had people rate themselves on a staggeringly long list of attitudinal items that related to how they lived, what they felt and thought about things, and how they did things. We were trying to get inside people's heads, to get at their secret thoughts, to understand the emotional or attitudinal reasons for responding to brands in a certain way. We also probed into people's outside interests to see if their life-styles reflected what was in their heads.

And sure enough, enough people behaved, thought, or felt in the same way that we could group similar people together and prove that there were unique and identifiable segments of life-style or personality clusters. We even gave the segments names, to capture the "essence" of the personality of members of the cluster. Sometimes we used famous people to personify the segments. For example, if one segment was labeled "Arnold

Schwarzenegger" and another "Danny DeVito," the differences between the needs and attitudes of these life-style segments would be instantly communicated. We found that each segment then became almost like a living, breathing human being that you could see with your mind's eye.

Learning From Mistakes

All this work was based on the hypothesis that if we could learn how and why people responded to things in general, we could predict how they would respond to specific things such as brands. We had translated the Badge Theory into a research hypothesis that was testable.

What we found, however, horrified us. There was no variability in brand shares across our life-style segments. "Arnold Schwarzenegger" bought the same brands, in the same proportions, as "Danny DeVito." In other words, general life-styles or personalities had nothing to do with brand purchase decisions. We couldn't use life-styles or personalities to position our brands because they weren't motivators for selecting one brand over another. Other market researchers in other industries were getting the same results: People-type groupings didn't predict brand purchase behavior in any product category. Our research hypothesis had to be rejected.

I was extremely upset about this at the time. I had just spent over $200,000 on the single largest piece of market research my company had ever done, and it hadn't given me the answers I expected. But once I had some time to reflect on the data, I started to see patterns that put the whole study into perspective. I saw, for example, that certain life-style/personality groups used our product class and others didn't use it at all. I also saw that some segments were heavy users of the product category and others were lighter users. Then it dawned on me: Measures of people types are better predictors of product-class selection than brand selection. In other words, life-style research is great for predicting whether a certain life-style segment will use the product category and how much of the product category different segments will use. However, life-style research cannot predict which brands will be used by the various segments because brands are often selected for brand reasons, not for people reasons.

The hypothesis that says that response to things in general leads to response to things in particular is flawed in at least four ways:

1. It doesn't take account of the effect of variations in the stimuli.
2. It doesn't recognize the environment in which the stimuli are received.
3. It doesn't recognize the consequences of acceptance of the stimuli.
4. It doesn't acknowledge the individuality of consumers.

These flaws can be illustrated by using the example of two brands within the product class of luxury hotel chains: the Hyatt Regency chain and the Mandarin chain. The people-types theory is flawed because it doesn't take into account the following considerations:

1. *Variations in stimuli.* The look and ambience of Hyatt hotels are very different from those of Mandarin hotels.
2. *The environment.* Some consumers may associate the Hyatt Regency chain with Yuppies and be turned off by that.
3. *Consequences of acceptance.* A consumer may not stay at a Mandarin hotel because it would upset her father, who is the manager of one of the Hyatt Regency hotels.
4. *Individuality.* The generalization may have nothing to do with a particular consumer's particular tastes, attitudes, and life situations.

So although it is safe to assume that upscale people are likely to stay at upscale hotels, you cannot use people types to predict which brand of upscale hotel a well-heeled consumer will choose to stay at. This is the ultimate WIFM issue: Brand superiority.

The Consequences of Confusing
Product Classes and Brands

There is little doubt in my mind that positioning brands on people types when they should be positioned on brand values has done more damage to brands in the 1970s and 1980s than any other factor. This is a major problem for marketers everywhere. Just look at television advertising and count the number of ads that attempt to motivate the consumer to buy the product class rather than a particular brand in the product class (almost all car and chewing gum ads, most soft drink and beer ads, fast-food ads, candy bar ads, and on and on). Thousands of marketers are using incorrect brand positionings because they have slavishly followed the Badge Theory/Brand Personality Theory of brand positioning without understanding that these positionings can be used only at the product-class level. Here's just a small sampling of the kinds of damage that can be done when you follow this brand-positioning strategy incorrectly.

Damage 1: Helping the Competition

Advertising the product class rather than a single brand stimulates demand for every brand in the product class. When a brand inadvertently positions itself as meeting the needs of the product class, it is essentially increasing the demand for all the brands in the product class, not just its own. That is OK for the top brand in the category, because any increase in overall usage of the category will disproportionately accrue to it. However, this is not a good brand position for the number-two or -three brand, because it unwittingly helps the competition more than itself.

Damage 2: Hurting Product-Class Sales

I worked in the beer industry for a number of years. It, like the cigarette industry, is constantly bombarded by consumer groups and government agencies complaining that beer advertising is essentially "life-style" advertising that makes beer drinking look glamorous and has a detrimental influence on impressionable under-age drinkers. Beer marketers deny this, claiming that the advertising merely tries to distinguish one brand from another, not influence people to drink the product class.

In my opinion, both sides are wrong. Today's beer advertising doesn't distinguish between brands, as the marketers claim. Much worse, it doesn't even sell the benefits of the product class, as the consumer groups claim.

Take a look at today's beer ads on TV. Couldn't you substitute a Bud for a Miller and get essentially the same message? Although some creative directors can truthfully claim that their ads are different because the casting and the setting are different, the central message that *most* consumers take away is the same for all brands: Beer and fun go together, especially when you are thirsty. Consumers are smart, and we should respect their intelligence, but that doesn't mean that beer drinkers can see the same subtleties of communication that advertising experts can. When the differences between brands are evident only in the minute details of casting, tone, mood, or setting, the marketers aren't talking to average beer drinkers—let alone talking to them in their own language. When consumers can see no difference between one beer brand's advertising and another's, what is there to be loyal to?

The beer example gets even worse because you can substitute most soft drink and chewing gum ads for beer ads and, other than the fact that the people in soft drink and chewing gum ads are younger, the main message is the same: The brand and fun go together. Beer advertisers are not selling the superiority of one brand over another; they are not even selling the superiority of beer over other product classes. So why would a consumer be loyal to the product class—beer—when the beer ads are no different from those of twenty or thirty product classes?

It is no wonder then that beer sales have softened significantly in the past few years. Some statistics that examined the correlation between beer advertising and total sales of beer showed conclusively that the more beer advertising there was on the airwaves, the more beer sales fell off. Although this study was done fifteen years ago, Paul Kohn of York University did a similar type of study in 1987. His conclusion was the same. To quote an article in the September 14, 1987, issue of *Marketing* magazine, "a high number of beer commercials tended to decrease men's beer drinking."

People are tired of beer ads that just show "pretty" people in "pretty" settings over and over and over. As a result, they use the product class less, either in protest against the advertising, or because beer commercials remind them of the Pepsi they have in the fridge. Since beer advertising does not give consumers a solid reason to be loyal to either beer brands or the entire product class, they decrease their loyalty to specific brands in the category, as well as use less of the category itself.

Damage 3: Merely Creating Awareness

Consider these two marketing "truisms": Much of today's advertising is designed to reinforce a consumer's predisposition to buy a brand. And, the primary purpose of today's advertising is to create awareness, not persuade consumers to buy. These are true statements based on a thorough examination of the kind of advertising being produced these days, but do we have to accept these principles? Wouldn't it be nice if advertising actually persuaded the uncommitted to buy? Or if awareness advertising could also tell people something so impelling that it would actually make them want to buy a brand? Why do we accept less than perfection as a rule of thumb in our business? I believe that many advertisers have used the Badge Theory/Brand Personality Theory of brand positioning in inappropriate circumstances and created these so-called truisms by accident, not design. Advertising that merely creates awareness uses people-type brand positioning when it should be using brand-value positioning techniques.

For example, a cigarette ad shows two couples smoking while enjoying a sail on an expensive sailboat. The ad is targeted at "Achievers" who need to buy expensive toys and wear high-quality brands on their sleeves to show their neighbors how successful they are. But the ad doesn't tell the consumer why this cigarette brand will impress the neighbors better than someone else's brand. It merely says, "I exist in this product class." That's about as motivating as the vacuum cleaner salesman saying, "My vacuum cleaner sucks up dust." All the advertiser is doing is getting the brand name in front of the public.

Damage 4: Not Even Creating Awareness

Awareness advertising is fine when launching a new brand or reminding consumers about a brand they may have forgotten. However, at some point, consumers want to know *why* a brand exists. That's what WIFM brand positioning is all about—to answer that simple consumer question. When the motivation for an ad is to satisfy the emotions of consumers, the result can be damaging for brands that have strong reasons for being, as this excerpt from a February 5, 1990, article in *Advertising Age* demonstrates:

> College students are no more confused than the general population when it comes to matching ads and brands.
>
> Several students chose the audiotape print campaign featuring the man sitting in the chair with his hair blowing back as their favorite print ad. The only problem for the marketer was that many misidentified the brand it advertised.

Take this test yourself. Which brand of audiotape is it? The answer is Maxell, but I would have incorrectly guessed Memorex.

One problem with positioning a brand based on people-type needs is that the needs are often so general that they can be fulfilled by hundreds of brands in hundreds of product classes. When this happens, the brand name doesn't register.

Another problem is a misuse of metaphors by people who create advertising. A metaphor is a figure of speech in which one word or phrase is used in place of another to suggest a similarity between the two. In advertising, a metaphor is the substitution of one image for another, in the hope that consumers will make the connection.

For example, I once developed a very descriptive profile of the person who drinks Bloody Marys. To summarize, she is a hedonistic and self-indulgent, but responsible and mature, upscale woman who is traditional, practical, has simple tastes, and demands quality in her brands because she likes to conspicuously consume. This creative profile is well executed in the Beefeater gin ad pictured. Unfortunately, an erroneous assumption has been made: that the same type of woman who likes Bloody Marys will also like Beefeater. The result is a lot of confusion and lack of brand-name registration.

By putting Beefeater in proximity to a well-executed person-ification of the Bloody Mary drinker, the advertiser is essentially trying to create a metaphor. Unfortunately, the reasons for drinking a Bloody Mary (the product class, in this instance) have nothing whatsoever to do with the reasons for buying a particu-lar brand of gin. The metaphor doesn't work because there is no link in the consumer's mind between the two parts. They are not perfect substitutes for one another because one image is at the product-class level and the other is at the brand level. Beefeater failed to close the loop and draw a link between the needs of product-class (Bloody Mary) users and the benefits of the brand of gin called Beefeater. This gives the consumer little incentive for brand loyalty and a real opportunity to forget the brand name.

If Beefeater had higher alcohol levels than other brands of gin, then a possible link could have been made between the higher alcohol level and the Bloody Mary drinker's tendency toward self-indulgence. Or if Beefeater was aged longer than its competitors, there could have been a link to the Bloody Mary drinker's need to impress others.

One of the acid tests of whether you are advertising the merits of a brand or the merits of a product class is to substitute a competitor's brand for your brand in one of your ads (or vice versa). If the message is exactly the same even though you've substituted brands, you haven't told the consumer why your brand is superior to the competition. In other words, you are doing product-class advertising and not making the link to brand superiority.

We could easily substitute a bottle of Gilbey's gin and change the headline to SO SPICY, SO GILBEY'S, with no difference in communication. The Bloody Mary is spicy not because of the gin but because of the spices in the mix. We can do the same with the footnote UNMISTAKABLY GILBEY'S. In fact, we could substitute

V8 for Beefeater or Gilbey's and the communication would probably be stronger and more believable.

The Beefeater ad actually says very little about the brand. In fact, the strategy behind this particular ad was to increase gin sales generally. Although gin sales have declined significantly in the past few years, Beefeater has been able to maintain or increase its share. The strategy of this campaign was to increase volume by getting Bloody Mary drinkers to substitute gin for vodka so that Beefeater could dominate a healthier, wider market. That's a sound strategy based on looking for WIFMs in contiguous product classes. But Beefeater forgot to close the loop and tell vodka drinkers *why* they should substitute gin in their Bloody Marys.

Lessons Learned

I learned from my work in life-style research that to focus on the general psychological needs of consumers is too simplistic and too narrow-minded in a product category where there is strong brand competition. Worse still is to base a brand's position on the examination of only one need type. The use of people-type needs as a marketing platform usually results in product class generalities rather than brand-specific needs. These generalities can result in either noncommunication or damage to brand or even product-class images.

The inescapable conclusion that you can't predict the specific from the general has broad implications for the many advertisers who use Badge Theory and Brand Personality Theory to position their brands. The most important implication is this: You shouldn't attempt to investigate WIFMs from the people-type needs side of the equation without looking at the needs-brands-satisfy side as well. Not only will brand values help you understand the customer better, brands themselves bring certain things to the purchase decision that cannot be measured from people types alone.

By not tying the brand value back to the customers' needs, advertisers don't close the logic loop for consumers and leave them with a message that is so general that it could apply to hundreds of product classes.

If nothing else, you must understand the difference between product classes and brands. Just because marketers have used Badge Theory and Brand Personality Theory too widely and mixed up product classes and brands when positioning their brands doesn't mean that we have to accept that brand loyalty is dead. Once the difference between product classes and brands is understood and demonstrated, Badge Theory and Brand Personality Theory will be able to take their rightful places in those positioning situations in which the marketer really wants to position a brand at the product-class level.

7

Finding Product-Class WIFMs

The ad for Kitty Litter is an excellent example of a WIFM at the product-class level. The basic need met by the cat-box–filler product class is the ability to manage cat waste so that it is not objectionable. Kitty Litter Brand hammers home its WIFM message with excellent visuals of a cat cozying up to a bag of the product in support of its strong tag line: THERE'S ONLY ONE KITTY LITTER. EVERYTHING ELSE IS JUST FILLER. The brand's WIFM is superior management of cat waste because it is *the only brand* that controls odors, dust, and odor-causing germs. And superior management of cat waste makes Kitty Litter Brand a must buy for consumers who want to know why they should buy this brand instead of another.

When trying to narrow the brand strategy to the one need that makes your brand superior to its competition, the place to start is at the product-class level—at the people-type needs as opposed to brand needs. Think of product-class WIFMs as benefits that a collection of brands provides to meet basic human needs. Although it is necessary to look at all the needs when searching for the one need to position a brand against, the search has to follow a logical sequence to reach the ultimate point: the WIFM for the brand.

NOW! *with* HEALTHGUARD™
Prevents Growth of
Odor-Causing Germs

99% Dust Free

There's only one Kitty Litter.®

Everything else is just *filler*.

Don't just fill your cat box when there's one cat box filler that can control odors, dust and odor causing germs, too. Only Kitty Litter® Brand has Healthguard.® It's sanitized to prevent the growth of odor causing germs while it absorbs both kinds of cat box odors. That's extra protection that you can't get from any other filler. And with a patented process, Ed Lowe's

Kitty Litter® Brand with Healthguard® is 99% dust free. Every time you pour Kitty Litter® Brand from the bag into the box, you get a clean, virtually dust free clay cat box filler that cats naturally prefer. Don't just fill your cat box. Deodorize, sanitize and clear the air of unhealthy dust. Buy the one that does all three ... Kitty Litter® Brand with Healthguard.®

It's the Ultimate Odor Controlor.™

Searching for the One WIFM

Step 1: Meet the Minimum Standards

The minute you enter a product class, there are certain minimum standards set by other companies in the product class that every brand has to meet. These minimum standards, often called price-of-entry or cost-of-entry variables, pertain to the ability of each brand in the product class to meet consumers' needs. If a brand does not deliver the benefits that meet these needs at the minimum accepted level, *as defined by consumers*, it is either not in the product class or doomed to failure. In other words, if the fanciest-looking, lowest-priced shampoo doesn't clean hair, it will fail.

Note, however, that as an industry matures, or as society becomes more sophisticated, consumer needs change. When Henry Ford first introduced the Model T, the basic human need that an automobile met was pretty simple and basic: Get me from point A to point B quicker than a horse and buggy. The first cars were, therefore, little more than motorized buggies. As the auto industry matured and consumers became more sophisticated, the minimum standards changed to include safety, a certain standard of design, basic creature comforts, and a certain degree of speed and reliability.

An astute marketer can often find a WIFM at the product-class level in a well-established industry where the leading companies have grown tired or sloppy, or they have been doing things the same way for so long that no one stops to question some of the basic assumptions of the business. The Japanese captured over 20 percent of the car market in a very short period of time by finding product-class needs that weren't being fulfilled in the U.S. marketplace.

Step 2: Define the Risks

What are the trade-offs (risks) a customer makes when using your product class over another? For example, a motorcycle driver accepts certain risks when he decides to use his bike instead of a car. It may be smart to use consumer market research to get the customers' perspectives, because even "experienced" people in the industry often can't see things from the consumers' point of view.

Risk reduction may be a useful WIFM in mature industries in which the principal competition has been doing things the same way for years. For example, the human needs that the beer product class fulfilled had not changed materially for over 2,000 years prior to 1974. Basically, the product looked and tasted the same, and it quenched thirst and provided "relaxation" as it had always done. With these benefits came certain risks for consumers who overindulged, such as getting drunk or having a beer belly. But these risks had long been accepted by beer drinkers everywhere as part of the definition of the product class. For most, the thirst-quenching and other benefits far outweighed the risks. However, as society began to change and ego needs took precedence over the more basic human needs (thirst quenching), a very intelligent U.S. brewer changed one of the risks by significantly reducing the calories in its beer. The rest is history, and today Miller Lite outsells its parent brand in many markets. Thus, as marketers change basic benefits (or risks, in this case), they are, in reality, defining a new product class or creating a subproduct class of the main class.

The Not-So-Sloppy-Joe sloppy-joe sauce ad pictured is another fine example of a new product that defines its WIFM in terms of risk reduction.

Step 3: Redefine the Product Class

If you got through the first step unscathed (and most well-established brands do), and you couldn't find a risk-reduction WIFM in step (2), then take a look at how you and your competitors have translated the basic needs for the product class into tangible things called brands. Don't take anything for granted. Question each piece of the product and see if there may be a better way of doing it. Do cars really need tires to get from point A to point B? Couldn't you clean dishes without using water? Does a beer have to be in liquid form—wouldn't powdered beer be more convenient? These kinds of questions can spawn whole

THERE'S ONLY ONE WAY TO SHOW YOU HOW THICK AND RICH OUR NOT-SO-SLOPPY-JOE™ SLOPPY-JOE SAUCE IS.

SO THICK YOU DON'T NEED A PLATE.

This sloppy joe sauce is thick and rich with a tantalizing hint of barbeque flavor. Just add it to your own freshly browned ground beef. Then, call the troops to the table and relax. Because Not-So-Sloppy-Joe™ sloppy joe sauce makes serving sloppy joes into a pretty neat experience.

new industries. And if you're successful, you can wipe out the current physical manifestation of your product class in one fell swoop.

If you haven't changed the delivery of the basic benefits (the price-of-entry variables) with your new invention, you don't really have a "better mousetrap," just a different one. That's a USP, not a WIFM. Remember, a WIFM at the product class level has to tell consumer why your brand is superior to every other brand in the product class. By starting at the product class level you are saying, "Here's why my brand is superior to the entire product class." Chances are that your invention changed some of the basic benefits and/or risks of using the product, or at least created a new subclass of the main category. How many offices still use manual typewriters or carbon paper? And how did we ever live without fax machines? Yet fax machines have been in common use for less than a decade.

The ad for the sugar-free Suisse Mocha flavor of General Foods International Coffees illustrates the subproduct class idea well. The parent class is, of course, coffee. Traditionally, coffee broke into two segments—regular and decaffeinated. Then an astute marketer realized that many people didn't like the taste of coffee and added flavored coffees as a new subclass. But this ad is interesting because General Foods has added a sub-subclass—sugar free. There's probably an opportunity for decaffeinated sugar-free flavored coffee as well.

Obviously, if you find something at the subproduct class level, you should stop your WIFM search and go with it.

Step 4: Look for a Competitive Weakness

The fourth step is to look at the list of major benefits of your product class and see if there is any one benefit that no competitor is delivering or claiming. If so, and you can demonstrate superiority in that area, then go with that product-class WIFM. For example, if Tide wasn't claiming and demonstrating that it cleaned clothes better than every other laundry detergent in the market and no other brand was saying it or doing it, there's your WIFM—as long as you can prove that you outclean them all. This is the brand-positioning area where Marketing Warfare

A cup of tenderness.   A cup of slenderness.

Our newest cup of tenderness has all the
fabulously rich, indulgent taste of our
originals with only 29 calories. Because
it's sweetened without sugar.

And, as well as our Suisse Mocha,
you can get our Cafe Irish Creme flavour
sweetened without sugar.

So now you can treat yourself to our
tenderness and keep your slenderness.

*Registered trademarks of General Foods Inc.
†NutraSweet and NutraSweet symbol are registered trademarks of
G.D. Searle & Co.

brand positioning is most fruitful. If you can find a chink in the leader's armor, you can capitalize on that weakness to win the war.

When to Stop at Product-Class WIFMs

If you haven't found a WIFM after taking the four steps above, you will have to enter the area of adding value to our brand offering by modifying the product, distribution, price, or one of the other brand values (this is discussed in detail in Chapter 8).

I can think of only six cases in which the marketer should attempt to use a WIFM at the product-class level to position a brand:

1. *Monopoly.* The brand is the only one in the category *and* it does not have direct brand competition from competing product classes. The Mazda Miata enjoyed this privilege for a short time until the Viper and others took a shot at the 1960s look-alike sports car market. With so much competition and deregulation of many of the utilities, it is difficult to think of more than a handful of instances in which a brand enjoys a monopoly situation. When you have a monopoly, however, it is appropriate to use the Badge Theory/Brand Personality positioning techniques, because your brand is essentially the product class.

2. *Brand Leader.* The brand is the leader in the category and has demonstrable superiority in the one basic thing the product class was designed to do. Although it is accepted marketing theory that a brand leader can use Badge Theory and Brand Personality Theory to take a leadership stance and therefore use life-style advertising to communicate this stance, I have the following cautions for market leaders that use life-style advertising for too long:

- The leadership stance may be perceived as arrogance or puffery by some consumers, who will abandon the brand merely because the brand was too big and egotistical.
- The brand may be so intent on communicating leadership that it forgets about modifying the more tangible market-

ing variables to keep pace with innovations or changing needs in the marketplace.

- The leadership stance had better cover *all* life-style segments that use the product class, or the advertiser will leave a hole in the target group that a competitor can lever to its advantage.

3. *Increasing primary product-class demand.* An industry association or brand is actively trying to increase use of the product class. Most industry associations have a mandate to increase primary demand for the product class, and many use advertising to increase sales of the basic product class. The Sugar Institute is a good example of the excellent use of a risk-reduction WIFM in its strategy. Remember the first time you heard that a teaspoon of sugar contained only sixteen calories? I haven't seen the statistics, but my guess is that sugar sales went through the roof.

4. *Weak Competitors.* All your competitors missed an important product-class motivator that your brand can meet better than any of them. This is a WIFM area that can yield tremendous market share, as the Japanese have taught us in many industries, but it is definitely not a strategy for the fainthearted. If the industry leader's marketers are asleep at the switch and your WIFM catches them napping, what are they likely to do? They'll jump out of bed with all guns blazing. This is marketing warfare at its finest.

I recently helped develop a new brand in a category in which the industry leader had gone to sleep. The leader hadn't had any real competition for a long time, and it showed. More importantly, however, was the fact that the market leader put all kinds of artificial ingredients and additives in its brand, which was supposed to be in a healthful product category. Most exciting of all, our market research uncovered that consumers knew that the leading brand was not as healthful as they wanted it to be. Our WIFM was laid out for us: Our brand was the only one that was really healthful. We captured sixteen market-share points the first year. But it wasn't an easy task, because the sleeping market leader woke up and tried just about every tactic possible to blow us away: prices lowered to break-even levels or below; advertising hyped to staggering levels; endless promotions; additional flavors added to the line; retail shelves packed and, where possible, our brand relegated to less visible positions; unheard of "deals" for retailers so they would favor the brand at the point of consumer contact. Despite this, 16 percent of the leader's franchise moved to our brand the first year—proof that an excellent WIFM can be found when the competition has been sleeping. But it's also proof that when you go head-to-head with a sleeping giant, you better have deep pockets and lots of patience, because when it wakes up, it will be a marketing war to end all wars.

5. *Risk Reduction.* You can use a product-class WIFM to demonstrate that your brand reduces the risk inherent in the use of the product class.

6. *A Better Mousetrap.* Your new invention has been able to change one of the major benefits of the product class.

Be extra cautious when you decide to use a product-class WIFM as your superiority claim, because product-class needs overlap; the same needs can be met by many product classes simultaneously. For example, the basic need for quenching thirst can be met by hundreds of product classes that have added benefits to the primary thirst-quenching benefit, subdividing the beverage product class into subsegments. The following table illustrates this point for six subsegments of the original thirst-quenching beverage product category:

Consumer Need	Coffee	Cola	Lemon-Lime	Bottled Water	Vodka	Beer
Liquid Replenishment	High	High	High	High	High	High
Refreshment	High	Low	Medium	High	Low	High
Warmth	Yes	No	No	No	No	No
Stimulation	Yes	Yes	No	No	No	No
Relaxation	No	No	No	No	Yes	Yes

This is market segmentation at its finest. If this table were completed, there would be hundreds of subproduct classes across the top and hundreds of needs down the side—thousands of permutations and combinations at just the product-class and subproduct-class levels.

The point is that marketers who have strong competition from a host of related product classes should steer clear of product-class WIFMs in claiming superiority. This also means stay clear of Badge Theory/Brand Personality Theory to position brands. It is almost impossible for a beverage or any other product that has a host of competitive product classes to claim that it meets product-class needs best. Banks also suffer from this problem because of the competition from other institutions that offer the product-class benefit of compounding interest. Similarly, airlines cannot advertise that they meet the basic need of the transportation product class: to get someone to a destination quickly. When you consider the commute to and from the airport, congestion in the airport itself, and the hassle of going through ticket vendors and security, taking a train, car, or bus may be quicker for short trips. It is not, however, unbelievable for a laundry detergent to claim that it can clean clothes best, because there is no competition in meeting this product-class need. Similarly, lawn mowers meet a need that no other product class can claim to meet.

When you examine today's marketplace, there are relatively few product classes that do not have strong competition from other product classes. Therefore, when product classes overlap or marketers cannot use product-class WIFMs, they will have to find a WIFM at the brand level.

8

Finding Brand WIFMs

After exhausting all possibilities of finding a WIFM at the product-class level, you move to the brand level to look for brand values that you can manipulate to better meet customer needs. Most marketers end up here because, with good competition and the overlap between product classes, it is difficult to find WIFMs at the product-class level. Brand WIFMs are those things that creative marketers and product developers add to their brands to increase their value or meet additional customer needs. There are fourteen of them, which were first listed in Chapter 5:

1. Sensory/performance
2. Quality
3. Durability
4. Ease of use
5. Packaging
6. Pricing
7. Availability
8. Variety of choice
9. Service
10. Healthfulness
11. Environmental friendliness
12. Popularity
13. Promotions
14. Advertising

The Search for Superiority

There are many product categories in which the sensory appeal
of the product itself is a primary benefit (the WIFM) to consumers. For example, the look of a car, the sound of a stereo, the
taste of a peanut butter, the feel of a moisturizing cream, and the
smell of a room deodorizer are critical factors that consumers
take into account when deciding to buy a brand or not. In many
categories, if the consumers' sensory receptors are not pleased,
the result is no sale.

The superiority of the product itself can be either a product-
class or a brand WIFM. If the product-class need is totally
dependent on the product's performance, the product itself can
be used as a product-class WIFM. An example of this is a lawn
mower, which only needs to cut grass evenly. This is a functional
need: The product performs a basic function that meets product-
class needs. When the appeal of the product is more an issue of
aesthetics or "form" than of function, the product can be used as
a brand WIFM because the design, smell, feel, taste, or sound of
the product adds value to how it performs its basic functions.

In most cases, it is relatively easy for product developers to
get a product to meet the basic needs of the product class.
However, as markets get more sophisticated, product development takes on a new dimension of adding extra value to the
product to make it more valuable to consumers. That's where
brand WIFMs come into play. As consumers become more sophisticated and as marketers become more creative in their
search for an edge over the competition, brands need value-
added features to keep them alive. With more and more market
segmentation, technological breakthroughs in virtually every
product class, and strong competition in most industries, it is
mandatory that you offer real, tangible brand values to consumers over and above the basic needs of the product class. In your
search for a brand WIFM, consider all the possibilities.

The Product Itself

Once again, it is relatively easy to start your search for your
point of superiority by just thinking about your brand as it now

exists. With a complete list of ingredients or components for yours and competitive brands, you can pretty much determine whether anyone offers a product-related brand value to consumers. Look at the physical makeup of brands in the product class. Do you offer a quality advantage that is exploitable? Can you support it as Chrysler did, by extending the terms of its warranty? The Volvo ad pictured tells people how its manufacturing process adds to the quality of its products.

Perhaps you can use technology to advantage to obtain superiority over the competition. Federal Express does this by using scanners to keep tabs on all packages in the system. This not only gives it a superior record for delivery, it also gives customers the assurance that if a parcel goes astray, Federal Express can find it easily. "When it absolutely, positively has to get there," says it all for this excellent WIFM marketer.

Is there an ingredient you use that makes your brand superior to competitors? For years, Coors beer has been stressing the fact that it is the only one to use pure Rocky Mountain spring water in its beer. Do you put purer ingredients and less filler in your brand than your competitors do? Kraft stresses this in its Kraft 100 percent grated parmesan cheese ad.

Do you do something better in processing your product that is of decided benefit to the consumer? Wiser's exploits this concept well by stressing that its DeLuxe whisky is aged for ten years. And it closes the loop nicely by telling consumers why extra aging meets the consumers' need for smoothness and superior taste. That's perfect WIFM advertising. Tell consumers you understand their needs, then tell them how your brand meets their needs better than every other brand.

Is your product more pleasing to the eye than a competitor's product? This is especially important now that form has surpassed function in many industries. Take electronics equipment, for example. Woofers and tweeters are still important, but now that stereo speakers have become a piece of furniture, we also think in terms of how that component will look in the room it will go in. The same goes for virtually every consumer product we buy. Certain colors are more eye-catching than others. That's why we use more yellows and reds on packages—to catch the consumer's attention. To my surprise, consumers can now buy garden

(*Text continue on page 101.*)

WHAT IF THE PEOPLE WHO BUILT YOUR CAR CARED AS MUCH ABOUT IT AS YOU DO?

for their work. And they wouldn't have it any other way.

This unorthodox approach has resulted in one of the best-built automobiles in the world today: the Volvo 760.

In the tiny town of Kalmar, Sweden—where all Volvo 760s are built—the assembly line as most people know it does not exist.

Here, people are not asked to perform small, repetitive tasks hour after hour like automatons. Instead, they work in teams assembling entire units of the car. Much of the work is done by hand. And the atmosphere resembles a workshop more than a factory.

Unlike many car workers, the "car builders" of Kalmar are rewarded not for how fast they build cars, but for how well. Here there is no anonymity. People are held responsible

A car you'll be proud to own. Because it's a car we're proud to have built.

VOLVO
A car you can believe in.

hoses in designer colors to match their houses. Who says form isn't as important as function in getting the edge on a competitor who's breathing down your neck?

Packaging

Is there something you can do with your container, from a functional point of view, that would make the consumer's job easier? Take your product home and go through the steps the customer has to go through: Unwrap it, pull it out of the package, if it has one. Notice any problems? Is there any way you can make the customer's job easier? When the Guinness beer people did this recently, they came up with a revolutionary new can. They found that the regular can suppresses the beautiful white foamy head that has become a trademark of Guinness over the years. So an engineer designed a can within a can. The larger can contains the beer. The secret to the foam is in the small can, which dispenses a small amount of gas once the entire unit is opened. Presto! Guinness beer that looks just like it does when the barkeep dispenses it from a keg down at your favorite local tavern.

But packaging can be more than just functional. Whole industries have been developed by thinking of vacations as all-inclusive packages that are so simple for the customers that all they have to do is pay their money and show up.

At the retail level, packaging can be approached another way. One innovative grocery store manager started to think about displaying his merchandise in "bundles" that equated with occasions-for-use in the customer's home. So he put all the barbecue supplies in one area, along with a generous display of steaks, barbecue sauce, plastic forks, and all the other grocery items needed to have a complete barbecue. This saved customers time running around the store hunting in the traditional areas for these items. It also increased the sale of the food items associated with barbecues because it was so much easier for consumers to purchase them.

The same type of thinking should be applied to the aesthetics of the container. One wine client spends a lot of time in this area because it knows that wine enhances an occasion, and for many, the enhancement starts when the bottle is put on the table.

Ease of Use

After examining the container your brand comes in, actually use the brand the way your customer uses it. You may find a dozen WIFM opportunities to make it easier to use your brand. One of the salad dressing brand managers probably went through this exercise to come up with the squeezable salad dressing bottle.

A pet peeve of mine, in the ease-of-use area, and one that offers an excellent WIFM for many manufacturers, is the wording of the owners' manuals. Some product manuals, especially those for electronics, are written in a language that is so foreign to the average consumer that it is a miracle consumers buy them. Computers are especially bad in this regard. I am convinced that the first computer manufacturer that sells the hardware with the software already loaded and ready to go, and then writes a simple step-by-step manual using lots of icons, will win the personal computer wars. Ease of use is a WIFM that is ripe for picking in this industry.

Customer service falls into the ease-of-use area for businesses that use service to add value to their main offerings. When you put yourself in the customer's shoes, you can often see opportunities to add or improve service. Many executives use their own brands, but they seldom purchase them the same way a regular customer does. So an executive for a car-leasing chain ought to line up at the ticket counter every so often just to feel what the customer feels. It wouldn't hurt to do the same thing at a competitor's counter. It may uncover a weakness that represents an excellent WIFM opportunity. One client of mine even has "secret shoppers" who do nothing but buy the company's products at every location where they are available. The buying process is then rated objectively, and the information is shared with the retailers. Needless to say, retail clerks are more likely to be on their toes when they think they might be being evaluated by a "secret shopper."

I discovered a new brand value WIFM in the service area (or rather, the un-service area) in the headline from a March 15, 1992, *Toronto Star* article: CAR DEALERSHIP FIRES ITS SALES FORCE—AND DOUBLES SALES. What this creative Florida car dealer did was fire the fourteen salespeople, fix the price of the cars, and offer them to customers on a no-haggle, take-it-or-leave-it basis. Not only did car sales double, the dealer's sales-related costs dropped 30 percent and, for the first time in a long time, the dealer is making a profit. Now that's taking advantage of the bad reputation of an entire industry.

Variety

While you are using your brand, think about how you can expand the line or offer consumers additional varieties. Most brands do this automatically if for no other reason than to give the product manager something new to talk about when communicating with consumers. Expanding the product line also tells consumers that the brand is keeping up with the times as well as keeping up with their need for more variety in their lives.

After-Use Factors

While you are using your product or service, remember to think about what happens after the use occasion. While browsing through a hardware catalogue, I noticed a new ladder that stores more compactly than a conventional ladder. This manufacturer found an after-use WIFM. I think minivans sold better than conventional vans because they fit in most people's garages better. No doubt they were the only vans to fit in underground garages for a while.

After-use is an untapped WIFM area that marketers often forget. Once again, put yourself in the consumer's shoes and think about what they do with your product or service after they use it. Do they dispose of it, store it, leave it where they found it, put it where they last used it, or cart it home from the office?

When considering products that are left in place after use,

think about how much space they take up. Making them more
compact or storable might be a good WIFM. I often think of the
waste of space when whole rooms are devoted to beds that are
used for only eight hours at night.

Popularity

Most marketers are surprised that I include popularity in WIFM
market research. This can be an extremely valuable WIFM for
the leading brand in a product class. Telling consumers that
yours is the leading brand or the biggest seller usually communicates that you are the best because you meet their needs better
than everyone else.

There are other aspects to popularity, however: There is
bigness itself, there is the aspect of growing in popularity, and
there is popularity among one's peers.

Growing in popularity is not used often as a brand positioning,
but it holds promise for aggressive marketers who want to tell
consumers that their brand is challenging the leader. Avis used
this approach with its extremely successful WE TRY HARDER campaign several years back. It's probably not a good idea to ever
announce that the brand grew to such an extent that it actually
became number one, however. The underdog approach elicits
sympathy from some consumers and gives them an additional
reason to buy, but once you become number one, the sympathy
angle is dead.

When a growing-in-popularity WIFM is used, it should be
accompanied by a firm statement about why the brand is meeting needs better than the leader. Growing in popularity then
becomes a secondary support to the main WIFM.

Popularity among peers works well in a select number of
product classes—beer, men's cologne, and cigarettes—in which
the brand purchase decision is a group decision rather than a
personal one. In other words, sociology drives the purchase
decision, not psychology.

Miller Lite used popularity among peers to great advantage
when the brand was first introduced. In actuality, what Miller
Lite represented, from a straight product point of view, was a

rather wimpy beer. After all, a "real man" would never admit he cared about calories or the filling properties of a beer, would he? Miller used the popularity-among-peers WIFM to sweep away any reservations beer drinkers might have about trying the brand by having the beer endorsed by indisputably serious beer drinkers from the sports world. This was excellent WIFM marketing that propelled the brand into first place in some beer markets almost overnight.

Healthiness and Environmental Friendliness

This area can include any major consumer trend that is fashionable, not just the environment. Virtually anything to do with a person's health or safety can be labeled topical these days, and the environmental cause is just another issue that stems from consumers' concern for their well-being. Lite/light everything abounds these days, as does anything to do with the three R's—reduce, reuse, and recycle.

Price and Promotions

In every market segment, there are at least three price need segments: regular price, premium price, and discount price. These three price positions offer excellent brand-positioning opportunities in virtually every product class.

Don't assume that everyone who uses your product class has a need for discount pricing. Those who need lower prices are usually a smaller subsegment of the product class, not the entire class itself. Discounting should be used only by those brands that position themselves against this subsegment. I am not a strong proponent of the wholesale use of price discounting or long-term price promotion as a value-added positioning to obtain a superiority edge over the competition. Heavy reliance on price discounting means that marketers are not meeting the needs of consumers in the regular and premium price categories.

There can be no argument that promotions have become the favorite tactic for moving brands off the shelves. Promotions now account for approximately two thirds of marketing budgets.

Spending on promotions grew from $32.7 billion in 1977 to
$109.5 billion in 1986; advertising grew from $23.4 billion to
$56.9 billion over the same period. That means marketers spend
almost twice as much on promotions as they do on advertising.
And the studies of the effects of promotions versus advertising
prove conclusively that promotions are much more effective in
moving tonnage. Some studies have even shown that promotions still outpull advertising, despite advertising's long-term
effects.

It's easy to praise promotions and assume that this tactic is
used so extensively because it meets consumer needs. But a
serious examination of the use of promotions as a brand's
primary marketing tactic suggests that promotions may not be
serving consumers well in either the short or the long term.

What consumer needs are coupons, price promotions, giving more product for the same price, and a host of other
giveaways meeting in today's marketing environment? Promotions are, in many cases, just creative ways to offer consumers a
discounted price.

Some will argue that promotions are more than price discounts, that they add extra value to a brand—and many do.
Some promotions are effective at enhancing the image of a brand
in the marketplace. A third way in which promotions are very
effective is in smoothing out seasonal variations in a brand's
sales by offering extra incentive for customers to buy the brand
in off periods. These are all effective ways to use promotions,
but these aren't the promotions I'm talking about. I'm talking
about the hundreds of thousands of promotions conducted each
year whose sole purpose is to discount the brand on a continuous basis. Contests can be included here, because from customer-
needs perspective, they are created to give the illusion that a
consumer can get something for nothing. So for clarity's sake, I
will call these types of promotions *price reductions*.

I have never seen an analysis of the frequency of the
different types of promotions used each year, but if my mailbox
is any example, price reductions must outnumber the other
types of promotions by a margin of ten to one. That concerns me
as a brand positioner, because I am left with an uncomfortable

feeling that in today's marketing world, price discounting pro-motions have become a new way to position brands. What started out as a short-term tactic has become, in many cases, a brand's entire positioning strategy.

Why have marketers let this happen? The answer is the brands themselves. A staggering number of brands don't have a WIFM, a Unique Selling Proposition (USP) or any demonstrable differentiating feature. Many are merely clones of the market leader ("me-too" brands). Others are erroneously trying to dif-ferentiate themselves on the life-style of the potential consumer rather than the superiority of the brand. Still others say nothing about themselves except that they exist. The heavy reliance on promotions probably came about because of the so-called mar-keting truism: It is difficult, if not impossible, to obtain real differentiation between brands in a competitive market.

Let's look at the price-reduction brand-positioning strategy from the customer's perspective. Consumers are pretty darned smart. When consumers can't see the differences between brands, they force marketers to give their brands away at a reduced cost. The smart consumer always goes with the brand that offers the lowest price, biggest discount, largest prize because there are no clear-cut advantages of one brand over another.

When price reductions are used as the primary marketing tool to differentiate one brand from another, it creates a market-ing system in which price discounting drives purchase decisions. Worse still, price is the only reason for brand loyalty. In this situation, loyalty is short term. Smart consumers buy your brand this week because you offer the lowest price, deepest discount, best coupon, biggest prize, or whatever. Then, next week, when your competitor out-promotes you with a better price discount, the consumers move to the competition. Loyalty lasts only until one competitor one-ups the other by offering a better discount.

With this going on, it must be clear to marketers that brand competition moves off the principle of fulfilling customer needs (the real brand-positioning issue) into the marketing tactics arena. What happens to brand images when price discounts become the strategy and the tactic? They suffer! Valuable brands start to look cheap in the consumers' eyes if discounts are too frequent or go on too long. Brands that use to stand for something substantial now stand only as tall as this week's promotion allows them to.

This suggests that when there is no demonstrable superiority of one brand over another, manufacturers have to give their brands away to prop up their market shares. However, if you are in a product class where there are substantial giveaways and discounts, look on the bright side: the opportunities for developing clear-cut superiority over the competition must be enormous. There are at least a dozen strong motivators for buying a brand other than price discounts—many of which are more important to consumers. Couldn't we obtain stronger brand loyalty if our brand outperformed the competition on what the brand was designed to do (wash clothes, cut grass, taste good, and so on)? Wouldn't a brand be more valuable to consumers if it were the only one to deliver a new packaging innovation that made the brand easier to use? Wouldn't a brand be more valuable if it offered better service? Add these to other brand-positioning variables such as durability, ease of use, distribution, variety of choice, healthfulness, environmental friendliness, and popularity, and you have an enormous number of brand-positioning alternatives other than price. And consumers have proved time and again that they are prepared to pay a reasonable price for value received.

Promotion Audits

Most marketers are good at conducting consumer assessments of creative advertising and packaging. Yet the one marketing tactic that seems to be gobbling up the largest amount of marketing dollars receives little in the way of auditing by brand marketers. My experience auditing a client's promotional program should be eye-opening.

I was hired to evaluate a multimillion dollar promotional program whose objective was to attract new users to the brand. The objective of the evaluation scheme quickly became a measure of how much new business was generated through the promotional program. In theory, the program would be good value to the company if the money spent on promotions was less than the amount of new business generated by the promotions.

I devised a consumer-based measurement scheme that essentially divided customers who had taken advantage of the promotions into three camps: new users of the brand as a result of the promotional scheme, regular users of the brand who took advantage of the promotion, and regular users of the category that flit from brand to brand depending on the promotions offered. What we discovered horrified us. Less than 1 percent of those who had taken advantage of the promotional program were new users of the brand. The remaining 99 percent were almost evenly split between what we termed "promotions shoppers," who buy whatever brand offers the best deal, and regular customers, who would have bought the brand without the promotion. The conclusion: The promotional program was adding very few new users.

Because of the way the program was evaluated, the client could calculate, to the penny, the true value of the promotional programs to the company. We showed him that several points of his market share were made up of consumers who will always buy the cheapest brand or the brand that offers the best deal because either they can't afford anything but the cheapest or they believe that all brands are the same (the discount price segment). Once he deducted the cost of losing these customers permanently from the cost of the promotional program, plus took into account the loss of margin from regular customers who were being rewarded for doing what they would have done anyway, the client realized that it would be money in the bank if he dropped the promotional program altogether. Efforts were then channeled in a new positioning direction based on giving the nonprice-driven consumer a more solid reason to be loyal to the brand.

I believe that many marketers would discover the same dismal news if they would take the time to audit their promotional programs. But I'm not holding my breath. I have already tried to get other marketers interested in this evaluation technique, with no success. With over $100 billion riding on promotions, however, it's about time someone raised some serious questions about this tactic, because the cost of promotions is really $100 billion *plus* the margin that is lost by offering loyal customers a discount.

Perhaps worse than the dollars spent is the fact that this one tactic accounts for two thirds of all marketing budgets. That's why I call it a strategy disguised as a tactic. When this much money is channeled into one marketing tactic (which is, in many instances, just a creative way to position a brand on price), price discounting must be the primary positioning strategy behind an awful lot of brands. This is fine if a marketer is sincerely trying to meet the needs of the small segment of consumers in a product class who are driven primarily by low prices. But any market segmentation scheme based on brand values will show that price is usually not the biggest factor when it comes to meeting consumer needs.

Using Promotions Wisely

Promotions are effective tactics in certain situations: to give a brand a short-term volume boost, to butter up retailers, to kick off a new brand, and to support a brand's positioning in the marketplace. Heavy promoting that relies solely on price discounting, however, is so easily copied by competitors that marketers cannot rely on this tactic alone to move tonnage over the longer term. Something more substantial than price discounting is needed to position the brand for the long haul, and that's where advertising can be used very effectively—to communicate the brand's position to consumers.

Advertising

When the dominant brands in any product category have product parity, packaging parity, the same level of quality and shelf life, equal pricing, roughly the same take-home distribution system, equal popularity, and promotions parity, the brands are stalemated until one uses one of the brand WIFM variables to break free of the pack. In product categories where the dominant brands have consumer-tested parity on all brand-value WIFMs, distinctive and superior advertising can be the edge that wins the market-share battle. But be sure that all brands are really equal in the critical area of product superiority, or no matter how good your advertising is, you will not become the market leader if a competitor discovers and uses its product edge as a WIFM.

Advertising is merely a tool to let consumers know that their needs are being met. The advertising itself is not the end goal from the consumers' perspective—the brand is. Advertising can never be as powerful a variable as the product itself. But when you've examined the other thirteen brand values without finding a WIFM, the heat has to be put on the advertising agency to outcreate the competition. However, I have never seen a case where a marketer had to rely solely on advertising as the WIFM. Stepping into the consumers' shoes and using the brand for a while should reveal other creative opportunities to bond consumers to the brand that are much more long-lasting than advertising.

No stone should be left unturned in your hunt for WIFMs at the brand-value level. Although it may seem terribly time-consuming to examine each of the brand values, for most brands it shouldn't take more than two hours to run through the list. It may be helpful to draw a chart that includes each of the brand values down the side and each of the brands (yours and the competition) across the top. Then fill in the matrix, being as objective as possible, to see where you or a competitor might have an edge. When you put your own and competitive brands under a microscope like this, some real surprises can jump out at you. However, don't rely only on your own internal evaluation of the extra value your brand offers over the competition. None of us can be completely objective. It makes good sense to get consumers to evaluate the various value-added elements on a regular basis.

Brand vs. Product-Class WIFMs:
The Cola Wars Example

The best way to illustrate the differences between product-class and brand WIFMs is the saga of the "Cola Wars." For years, the cola companies treated colas as "image" products and touted the virtues of the product class as a reason for drinking their brands. Colas are probably the best executors of Badge Theory in marketing today, Even the second- and third-place brands use Badge Theory, product-class advertising in their respective subsegments.

When I questioned several advertising executives about why the colas did only life-style advertising, their response was that because there is so little difference between the taste of brands in the cola category, it was necessary to differentiate the brands on "imagery." In other words, differentiating brands on the basis of their "image" will result in the consumer wearing the brand like a badge—the Badge Theory argument.

Such beliefs resulted in slogans and pictures that showed young people having fun in the sun on the assumption, I guess, that one cola goes better with fun or volleyball or whatever than another cola. This is pure people-type positioning at the product-class level; it ignores the fact that there is so much competition between colas that there has to be brand differentiation on one or more of the brand values. Badge Theory suggests that one brand meets general product-class needs (fun and refreshment) better than another brand. The flaw in the argument, of course, is that it's just not true. One cola cannot go better with fun and refreshment than another cola. Indeed, there are those who will argue that you can have more fun with beer than with cola.

What the colas were doing, in essence, was awareness advertising that sold the benefits of drinking colas (or almost any brand of soft drink) rather than the benefits of one cola brand over another. Some have argued that it is absolutely correct for the market leader, Coke, to take this position, because product-class advertising is a leadership stance that basically says, "We are better at meeting your needs than every other brand in the category, and the proof is that we are the leading brand."

The flaw in this leadership-stance argument, in this case, is that Coke could not demonstrate superiority in meeting one of the most important and basic consumer needs: taste preference. Although it may be OK for market leaders to take a leadership stance, it is the kiss of death for a market leader to do this without covering its behind in the critical area of sensory/ performance superiority.

Eventually, someone got the WIFM message, because one day a cola did some brand WIFM investigating and discovered why one brand of cola was superior to the other. That cola said, "This brand tastes better, and a brand-blind, paired comparison taste test is the proof." Score one point for Pepsi for finally telling consumers why they should buy one cola over another and respecting consumers' ability to discern and appreciate the difference in taste between the two brands. Pepsi also said, "Our cola tastes so much better that people are switching away from the competitor at a rapid rate." Score two points for Pepsi for distinguishing itself from its competitor on a brand WIFM (the popularity of one brand over another), and for appealing to the consumers' need to know that they are not alone in appreciating the taste superiority of Pepsi.

Then Pepsi's competitor made a huge mistake—it changed its formulation. Pepsi jumped all over this by saying, "See, we've been telling you all along that we tasted better, and Coke has just confirmed it." Score three points for Pepsi for appealing to the honesty of consumers.

What I cannot believe, however, is that after all this astute marketing, following the WIFM philosophy, and recognizing the differences between brand and product-class WIFMs, Pepsi is once again doing Badge Theory commercials in which you could substitute Coke for Pepsi and get the same message. Didn't Pepsi learn that if there is an honest difference between major brands (and there always is), consumers want to know about it? Consumers have proved to Pepsi, by their brand-switching behavior, that they will reward the brand that meets their needs better than the competition and can prove it.

Pepsi proved in a blind taste test that it tasted better than Coke. Coke admitted it and changed its formulation. Then Coke was forced by consumers to reintroduce the original Coke because consumers didn't like the new formulation. So what did Pepsi do with this marvelous marketing opportunity that it both created and fell heir to due to the marketing behavior of its chief rival? It went back to doing generalized product-class, Badge Theory advertising again that just says, "Pepsi belongs to the same product class as Coke." Pepsi even copied Coke and hired rock stars to sing about its brand.

Pity the poor consumers in the middle of all this. They had proof that one cola met their needs better than another. Then the one that said it was better got outmaneuvered for an instant by the competitor, which reintroduced the original formulation. The logical question for consumers to ask was, "Is New Coke now as good as or better than Pepsi?" And Pepsi's nonresponse was to give them the old young-people-having-fun-in-the-sun stuff.

Pepsi had been winning the game, but it just dropped the ball and stopped playing. By not answering Coke's challenge, Pepsi as much as confirmed that it is not better than New Coke and there is no longer a solid reason to buy Pepsi over Coke. In one stroke of the advertising pen, all Pepsi's advantages were wiped out. What a shame! Consumers were really interested in the differences between the two brands.

Pepsi had many optional moves it could have made to counteract Coke's reintroduction of Coke Classic. Pepsi could have told consumers that original Pepsi was preferred to both Classic and New Coke in blind taste tests, if indeed that were true. Or Pepsi could have introduced a New Pepsi that beat New Coke in blind taste tests. Or Pepsi could have confirmed that Pepsi was continuing to grow in popularity, despite all the maneuvering by Coke. Or Pepsi could have told people that taste tests confirmed that the taste of New and Classic Coke was so similar that people couldn't tell the difference, if that were true. If nothing else, Pepsi could have continued to use the Pepsi Challenge brand position, because the introduction of New Coke didn't alter the fact that Pepsi still beat Coke Classic in a brand-blind taste test.

Perhaps Pepsi didn't make these moves because it believed what the so-called industry experts were saying about consumers getting tired of the Cola Wars. It's unfortunate for consumers that Pepsi didn't respond to the challenge. Confusion on the taste issue has made the buying decision more difficult for consumers.

Product Testing

The longer I am in marketing, the more I am convinced that what the consumer can see, feel, smell, taste, and hear (rather than the generalized personality of the brand or product class) accounts for close to 100 percent of the reason they select one brand over another. Yet one of the most important brand WIFM questions manufacturers forget to ask is, "Is there one brand in the category that is superior to all the others in a brand-blind product test?" Many manufacturers assume product parity when it isn't necessarily true. This is especially tragic when demonstrable product superiority is a primary motivator in brand selection, as it is in most categories. To ignore product superiority could mislead the manufacturer into placing emphasis on less important consumer needs when a strong product-related WIFM is what is really needed.

Perhaps your product can be altered slightly to achieve product preference. If so, do it and claim it as your WIFM. The Kao Soap Company has been very successful in this area by continually changing formulations to keep its brands superior to the competition. This is evolution, not revolution, and every brand in every category has to do this just to stay alive in today's competitive marketplace.

Many marketers are reluctant to talk about their brand's superiority in taste, performance, or design. Perhaps the reason for this is that marketers have been trained to deal primarily with brand values, which include such factors as pricing, packaging, distribution, advertising, and promotion but they have not been trained to look at other variables of the mix—especially the product itself.

I've heard marketers use the "taste has no memory" argument as a reason for not doing paired comparison, brand-blind product tests. I don't believe this argument, especially in product categories that are ingested on an almost daily basis. In fact, I have had to build controls into product tests to eliminate the bias as a result of taste familiarity in certain product classes. Otherwise, the leading brand would always have been first in the product test simply because there were more leading-brand users in the sample.

I am an advocate of rigorous product testing, and it is vital if you are claiming the high ground of product superiority. Be careful, and don't forget that the consumer is intelligent. If you aren't able to substantiate your product superiority claim, it will buy you massive trial, but no retrial. Schlitz beer shot itself in the foot by claiming taste superiority at the same time it was cheapening its product.

Even if your market research group tells you that you currently have a superior image rating on "tastes best," don't move your brand position into this territory unless you have demonstrable superiority in a brand-blind consumer product test. A brand-image statement like "tastes best" doesn't relate to taste at all. It is merely a consumer expression for "I like it best" or "it is my favorite." In other situations, brand images can lag the real world by several months or years. In these cases, a brand may have taste preference perceptually, but because a hungry competitor has been modifying its product, the competitor may actually have preference in a brand-blind paired comparison.

The reason for differences in taste perception between a brand-blind product test and a so-called product test in which the brand is identified to respondents is that by telling consumers what the brand is, you are no longer isolating the product variable. Therefore, you are not doing a product test at all. You are doing an image test, because you are letting the brand influence the answer to the product question. When you tell consumers what the brands are in a brand-identified taste test of soft drinks, for example, one consumer may answer the taste question honestly, but another may be thinking, I prefer the taste of the Pepsi they just gave me, but I really hate Pepsi's advertising, so I'm going to tell them that I prefer the taste of Coke.

When you don't give research respondents a clean and unbiased question to answer, you cannot deduce a clear answer from the results. To then conclude that taste is not important because it can be influenced by imagery is a fallacy. Taste is taste, and it cannot be modified by imagery. It can be lessened in importance by imagery or modified in some way by some more overpowering stimulus (for example, aroma). Only if a product test is done correctly and you have truly isolated the product component can you measure its importance in the entire scheme of marketing variables.

Listening to Consumers

In every nonretail product category I have worked in, be it newspapers, government services, or image products like alcoholic beverages and personal care products, *product acceptance* is the primary reason for selection of one brand over another. Because of the importance of the product variable, you should use one of the other brand values as your brand WIFM only when you cannot possibly achieve product superiority.

If you believe that consumers are as intelligent as I do, you will have reached the conclusion that they will get to know, in time, which brands are good and which brands are bad. Consumers don't get to try brands in paired comparison product tests very often, but they do talk to each other and are forever comparing the merits of one brand over another. Sometimes consumers can see the merits of another brand just by walking around the neighborhood (her laundry looks cleaner than mine, or his lawn mower seems to cut a lot more evenly than mine). This often results in the consumer trying a competitive brand. This informal test is, of course, biased by brand imagery, but millions of consumers are doing it every day. And you haven't got a chance if your brand doesn't beat the pants off the neighbor's brand in this less-than-rigorous comparison. Not only can't you substantiate your claim, the consumer now has a second benefit for switching brands—the social acceptability and good feeling that comes with doing what others are doing (a popularity WIFM).

What the Cola Wars pointed out to me is that consumers are a lot smarter than we give them credit for and over the years I've had this confirmed many times. For example, I've seen consumers dump on me-too brands simply because they were me-too and didn't offer any tangible benefit over the brand they were copying. Who says the consumers aren't intelligent?

Nor do the so-called experts always know what they are talking about when they tell us that they are speaking on behalf of some major influence group. For example, a domestic winery had come to believe what wine snobs everywhere were saying about nonimported wines: that wine consumers thought domestically produced wines were poor in quality compared to French or German wines. The domestic wine industry believed this to such an extent that it even priced its wines significantly lower than the import competition. In a landmark piece of research, this winery was pleasantly surprised to find that over half of wine drinkers were extremely satisfied with domestically produced wines and preferred them to imports—rating them best for value received.

Another example of the experts being dead wrong is the case of a relatively new baseball team that was doing miserably on the field. The media fanned the flames by stating that they were speaking on behalf of baseball fans everywhere when they called for the hiring of several superstars to turn the team around. Solid market research proved, however, that real baseball fans didn't want superstars, especially when they found out they'd have to pay for the substantial cost of this solution through much higher ticket prices. So the team listened to its customers and stuck to its strategy of developing promising players from within and keeping ticket prices low. Guess what happened? The Toronto Blue Jays went on to win the division championship a few years later and recently won it again. Who says consumers aren't smart?

I've seen many examples of consumers telling manufacturers how they can improve a brand to make it better. In many cases, the manufacturers have listened. Unfortunately, in those few cases in which the manufacturer didn't listen, it paid a substantial price in both lost market share and lost revenue.

When manufacturers don't take consumers into their confidence and treat them as equal partners, it's because they don't have confidence in the consumers. For example, when consumers couldn't find substantial superiority of one brand in a home placement product test, they were labeled "stupid." It didn't occur to the manufacturer that it was in charge of creating tangible product superiority, not the consumer. In other cases in which an "obviously well-targeted and well-executed ad" was panned by consumers because it failed to communicate a message, the consumers were labeled "tasteless."

If nothing else, over the past twenty-five years of new product development work I've learned that consumers are a lot smarter than we give them credit for. Perhaps it's our own lack of confidence in consumers or our own insecurities about our abilities to create and market better and more carefully targeted brands that have held us back. I know from personal experience that when you assume an equal relationship with your consuming public, walk in their shoes for a while, and offer them good brands with tangible benefits, you will win the marketing war. To do less is a disservice to them and to yourself.

Every marketer should conduct an objective consumer product test as the first step in determining brand WIFMs. This will help you determine whether your product meets the sensory and/or performance needs of consumers in your product class. And you might be pleasantly surprised at how well your product performs against its competition.

That's not to say that product superiority alone will win the marketing war. But, the brand that has parity on the non-product-related brand-value WIFMs and superiority on the product-related brand WIFM will be the market-share leader.

9

Corporate WIFMs

From a company's point of view, there are three major areas where WIFMs can come from: (1) the product-class needs that the company's products have to fulfill to even compete in the product class, (2) the value-added brand WIFMs that make one company's brand superior to another's, and (3) those unique features of the corporation itself that add or subtract from the overall acceptance of its brands. These latter corporate-driven variables usually make up the corporation's philosophy and include such things as the ownership of the corporation, its attitude toward its customers, its attitude toward the industry it's a part of, its size and market position, its stand on national or international issues, and most recently, its position on environmental issues. The following variables usually show up in some type of corporate image statement:

Ownership

• Private
• Public

Attitude Toward Industry

• Act as industry leader
• Hold prices down

Attitude Toward Customer

- "King" or "peasant"
- Know customers best
- Open and honest

Attitude Toward Employees

- "Knights of Round Table" or "serfs"
- Part of team or independent
- Open and honest

Magnitude

- International role
- National versus regional
- Major versus minor
- Bigness

Success

- Profitability

Nationalism

- Create/keep jobs in country
- Domestic versus foreign ownership
- Reduce dependence on imports
- Keep dollars in country
- Protection from foreigners

Issues Stance

- The environment
- Employment equity
- Corporate persona
- Charitable contributions

If you've got lots of dollars and time on your hands and feel that you've established all the product-class and brand WIFMs you can, you might want to look for a WIFM at the corporate level.

I am not a strong proponent of corporate WIFMs because I believe that to most consumers, a corporation is merely the sum of its brands or is some huge, faceless, unapproachable mass. Years of market research at the corporate level of multibrand companies has left me with the solid conviction that the consumer does not buy corporations; it buys brands.

That's not to say that corporations aren't taken into account when some brands are bought—for example, when the brands of the corporation have a long history of success in meeting consumer needs. But that doesn't mean that the corporation has to promote itself as a corporate entity. The work I have done with corporations and brands suggests that all the corporation needs to do is continue to deliver brands that truly meet consumer needs, and the corporate reputation will follow.

Before you start your search for corporate WIFMs, complete the following sentence: The company I work for is called _____ and the consumer drinks/eats/rides/uses/applies/wears/etc. my brand called _____. If the name you write in each blank is the same, there is no need to look for corporate WIFMs, because the brand and the corporation are interchangeable in consumers' minds. Some large companies forget this, and when they try to launch a whole new product line under the corporate name, it fails. Xerox is the classic example of this phenomenon. Xerox and copiers were the same thing to consumers. In fact, the brand and the product class were so powerful at the consumer level that when you mentioned copy machines, the consumer automatically thought Xerox, and vice versa. Copies became known as Xerox copies, and secretaries were told to make a Xerox of something whether the copy was run on a Xerox machine or not. So when Xerox introduced a line of computers under the Xerox name, it was, not surprisingly, a failure. To consumers, Xerox had nothing to do with computers. Not only was Xerox not telling consumers what was so superior about its computer that they should buy it over IBM's; it was mixing computers with copying machines.

The current trend toward branding retail outlets is recognition of the fact that the brand and the corporation are generally one and the same at the retail level. Therefore, a retailer who recognizes that it can use brand WIFMs to distinguish itself as superior to other retailers in the same industry is not a whole lot different from the product manager who does the same thing with brands in the packaged-goods field.

Only after you have established that the brand and the corporation are separate can you legitimately look for corporate WIFMs. There are three areas where corporate WIFMs can be generated:

1. When you have a legitimate corporate superiority that will make consumers more receptive to your brand line.
2. When you have a corporate image problem that would hamper consumers from making positive decisions about your brands.
3. When your competition has a corporate image deficiency that would make consumers think twice about buying any of its brands.

Legitimate Corporate Superiority

Corporate WIFMs tell the consumer why your corporation is so superior to the competitor's corporation that they should buy your brands rather than its brands. I could find only one legitimate corporate WIFM in the hundreds of advertisements I examined to find examples for this book.

What I found were very nice and often catchy statements about a company that were so general that you could easily interchange competitors' names. For example, Anheuser Busch's slogan of a few years back, SOMEONE STILL CARES ABOUT QUALITY, is true of Anheuser Busch, but it is also true of many other companies—beer and otherwise. When a corporate slogan can apply to hundreds of corporations in hundreds of industries, it is not a statement about the superiority of one company over another, and it does not help consumers make better buying decisions.

I keep looking for true corporate WIFMs in advertising, with little luck. Here's a smattering of current corporate slogans. Try to guess what the company is, or even the product class (answers are below):

1. EXPERIENCE YOU CAN TRUST
2. WE CARE ABOUT THE SAME THINGS YOU DO
3. IN TOUCH WITH TOMORROW
4. EXCEPTIONAL PERFORMANCE
5. THE RELENTLESS PURSUIT OF PERFECTION
6. WE GO FARTHER FOR YOU
7. FOR THE WAY IT'S MADE

None of these slogans is a corporate WIFM because the company has not told consumers why it is superior to its competition. Each has a strong message about caring for customers or about one of the driving factors behind the company, and these are good things to know about a company. However, most consumers could think of dozens of companies with the same attributes. If a corporate slogan doesn't meet the WIFM rule of *superiority,* it doesn't offer consumers any motivation to make a buying decision in a company's favor.

The one corporate WIFM I found was a TV advertisement for General Motors, which stated that GM sells more cars than its two nearest competitors combined. This kind of success is a meaningful motivator to a large portion of the population that knows GM got to be this big because it has been delivering good products for a long time. This corporate WIFM tells consumers that because GM has met their needs better than its competition for so many years, consumers have made it the most popular company in its industry.

Corporate Deficiencies

There are many instances of companies being ruined by corporate image deficiencies. This is one place to look for corporate

Correct Answers: (1) Persian Carpet Centre, (2) Scott Paper Company, (3) Toshiba, (4) Hitachi, (5) Lexus, (6) Hertz, (7) KitchenAid.

WIFMs. First, make sure that your company doesn't have any *major* flaws in the eyes of customers for your product class. These usually show up in consumer market research when the consumer says: "I wouldn't buy any brand that company makes because. . . ." Several large stockbrokers whose employees were caught with their hands in the till found themselves in this position during the "greedy eighties."

Sometimes a corporate deficiency rears its ugly head unexpectedly and produces massive long-term effects that are hard to erase. Exxon's oil-spill problems in Alaska and Perrier's filter problems will probably haunt these companies for years to come. However, many of the problems in this area stem from rumors that one competitor circulates about another. This is a terrible way to do business, and it is both immoral and illegal. Unfortunately, it happens all too often. And these kinds of rumors are hard to snuff out, especially with something that is consumable.

To this day I still avoid a certain hamburger place because when I was a child someone told me they used ground cat meat in the hamburgers. Now I knew that this was preposterous, and all logic told me that the place wouldn't have been in business for so long if it did. But, every time I went there, I thought about ground cats. The company never addressed the rumor in a positive manner.

Dow Chemical, the marketer of the top-selling consumer food wraps Saran Wrap and Handi Wrap, also chose to ignore a corporate image problem. Over the years, Dow has been criticized for its involvement in the production of war-related products. But Dow presumably discovered that an antiwar boycott of its products would not affect the food wrap line, because most purchasers of food wraps don't know who makes them. This is one instance in which having a low corporate profile on brands paid off. In this instance, addressing the corporate image deficiency at the consumer level would probably have just fanned the flames unnecessarily.

Sometimes, however, corporations ignore persistent problems until consumers tell them, through lawsuits or at the cash register, that they are fed up. This happened to the two car giants Chrysler and Ford. Ford ignored its "rusty Ford" image for so long that sales were hurt and it attracted lawsuits from disgruntled customers. In addition to correcting the rust problem, Ford now uses the corporate slogan QUALITY IS JOB ONE as a backdrop to its entire brand line. This is not a WIFM statement, however, since Ford does not tell consumers that it is superior to its competition on the issue of quality. However, the statement provides assurance that the company has cleaned up its act, and this is useful information for consumers to know.

Chrysler's problem became well known following its massive financial bailout by governments on both sides of the forty-ninth parallel. Chrysler changed the course of its history by introducing well-made, contemporary models that competed head-on with the aggressive Japanese imports and pulled itself out of the mire. Chrysler's corporate slogan changed from the "bailout" days slogan, DRIVING TO BE THE BEST, to the current slogan, BUILDING TO BE THE BEST. Chrysler's new corporate statement is not a true WIFM because it doesn't say why Chrysler is superior to Ford or General Motors. It is, however, an excellent overall statement about its business philosophy. Presumably, the most recent change expresses the company's strong desire to communicate the quality of its product line more than its need to tell consumers how aggressive it has become. Perhaps this shift in corporate thinking is why Chrysler has not been doing as well in the marketplace. The customer is still stuck with a brand decision: Why should I buy a Chrysler New Yorker over a Buick Park Avenue?

Competitive Corporate Deficiencies

The third way to look for corporate WIFMs is by checking out the image of competitors and looking for corporate deficiencies that would turn customers off. If you find one, however, it is often better to turn that deficiency into a positive for using your company's brands, rather than putting the competitor down directly. After all, you don't want consumers to choose your brands by default.

Sometimes problems with a single brand can affect the entire corporate lineup, especially when the company specializes in only one product. For example, the story about the Suzuki Sidekick rolling over when turned too sharply could have turned many people away from buying any Suzuki. I really have to take my hat off to the creative marketer who turned lemons into lemonade on this issue, however, by advertising a free crash helmet with every Sidekick sold.

Mixing Corporate Slogans and WIFMs

Most often, corporate slogans are used as a backdrop to brand WIFMs. For example, the Beatrice Corporation used to put a tag line on each of its brand ads that stated, ANOTHER QUALITY PRODUCT FROM THE BEATRICE CORPORATION, suggesting that everything the company does is first class. This slogan may not make consumers buy Beatrice ice cream over Sealtest, but when a company has lots of money, this type of slogan is good insurance against future rumors. If nothing else, Beatrice's corporate slogan gave consumers more confidence in the company behind the brands. And if the burger chain I went to as a kid had said all along that it used only 100 percent pure beef in the hamburgers, the ground cat meat rumor would never have taken hold.

There can be little doubt that when consumers buy brands, the reputation of the company has a lot to do with their selection of one brand over another. Companies such as Sony, Gillette, and General Foods have been delivering high-quality products for such a long time that we are more likely to buy brands from these companies than companies that have no proven track record. But that's not the WIFM issue. The issue from the consumers' perspective is: Tell me why your corporation is so superior that I should buy your brands rather than your competitor's. That's a hard question for many corporations to answer because at the corporate level there probably aren't a whole lot of differences. Most differences occur at the brand level.

Therefore, corporate WIFMs work best when they are used as a backdrop to specific brand WIFMs. In this case, the manufacturer is usually making a blanket statement about the corporate philosophy that will make consumers sympathetic to the entire brand line. However, unless the corporation has a unique feature that makes it superior to every other corporation in that industry in meeting consumer needs, it is generally a waste of time and dollars to look for corporate WIFMs. Or, unless you have corporate image deficiency or you can exploit a competitor's corporate image problem honestly, there is little point in doing corporate WIFM advertising.

10

WIFM Hunting

By following the WIFM system in sequence, you are narrowing down the brand-positioning possibilities to the *one* need that your brand fulfills better than the competition (the WIFM), as you can see from the following diagram:

The WIFM System

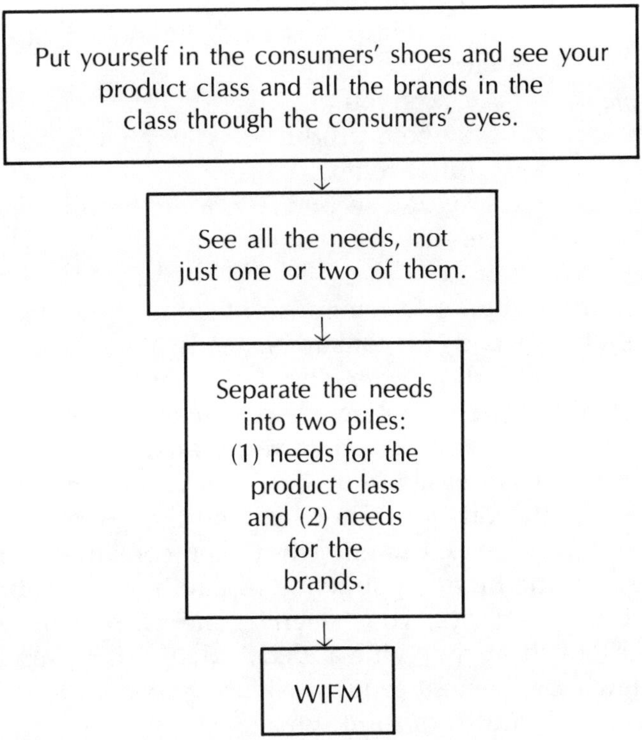

Put yourself in the consumers' shoes and see your product class and all the brands in the class through the consumers' eyes.

↓

See all the needs, not just one or two of them.

↓

Separate the needs into two piles: (1) needs for the product class and (2) needs for the brands.

↓

WIFM

All this may seem overwhelming at first, but it needn't be. In many cases, if you just think about the components of the product, you get a pretty good fix on consumer needs at the product-class or price-of-entry level. Take beer, for example. The amber liquid in the bottle is a bitter, cold liquid made from natural grains that when fermented turn to sugars and a drug that depresses the central nervous system. What needs are met by such a product? Let's take the pieces of our description and see:

Liquid:	• Replenishes lost body fluids
Bitter:	• Usually relates to the thirst-quenching properties of a liquid
	• Is a product risk in that it may turn people off it it's too bitter
Cold:	• Refreshes when you are thirsty
Natural:	• A healthy product
Sugar:	• A nutritive
	• May be a product risk because it can be fattening
Alcohol:	• Relaxes you
	• May be a product risk because it can inhibit natural reflexes
	• May be a second risk at the product-class level because it is addictive

With little more than a few minutes of think time, the benefits and risks of beer and the consumer needs it fulfills come tumbling out. So far it didn't cost you a cent and you have uncovered most of the product-class needs you will have to take into account to position your brand correctly at that level.

Once you have based your thinking purely and simply on consumer needs, you will want to expand the exercise, for three reasons: (1) you haven't defined from the consumers' perspective whether one brand is superior to another in meeting their product-class needs, (2) you haven't gone beyond the product class and looked at the value-added benefits that brands offer, and (3) few management groups will accept a brand positioning based on two minutes of think time.

Expanding the Search

Phase 1: In-House Data

Most consumer-driven companies have a wealth of information in-house to get you started on your WIFM hunt. Search the files for information about when, where, and how your product class is consumed; where it is purchased; the types of people that use it; the existence of subsegments of the product class; what specific needs the subsegments fulfill; who the major players in the category are; why they seem to be doing well; whether they have any exploitable weaknesses; and so on.

After you have been through this exercise, you will have completed the first step in the brand WIFM process as shown in Figure 10-1.

Phase 2: Consumer Verification Through Market Research

At this point your thinking has generated hypotheses that may or may not be correct. So now is the time for you to do some objective, external testing of your hypotheses through the conduct of well-executed market research. This phase calls for the quantification of the various WIFMs that are out there. And since you've already read Chapters 7 and 8 on finding WIFMs at the product-class and brand levels, you know what types of measurements you need to use in order to find WIFMs in your product class.

Defining the Product Class Correctly

Whole books have been written about how to arrive at a company's "mission," but that is essentially what you must do when you are defining WIFMs. Markets have become so fragmented that the traditional way of defining markets, in terms of similar companies in the industry, has broken down. Your Phase 2 research must be conducted in the context of everyone you compete with, not just the traditional ones. For example, banks now compete with trust companies, savings and loans, credit unions, insurance companies, real estate companies, and invest-

Figure 10-1. The brand WIFM process.

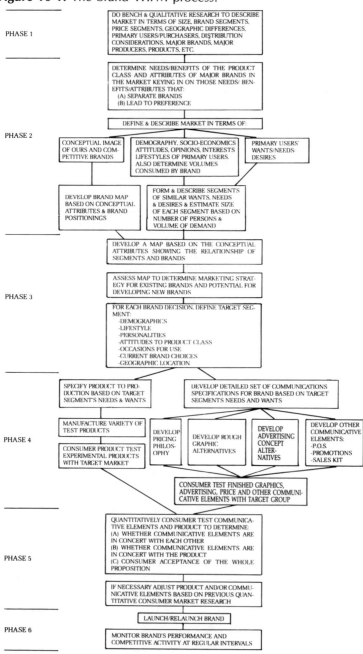

PHASE 1

DO BENCH & QUALITATIVE RESEARCH TO DESCRIBE MARKET IN TERMS OF SIZE, BRAND SEGMENTS, PRICE SEGMENTS, GEOGRAPHIC DIFFERENCES, PRIMARY USERS/PURCHASERS, DISTRIBUTION CONSIDERATIONS, MAJOR BRANDS, MAJOR PRODUCERS, PRODUCTS, ETC.

DETERMINE NEEDS/BENEFITS OF THE PRODUCT CLASS AND ATTRIBUTES OF MAJOR BRANDS IN THE MARKET KEYING IN ON THOSE NEEDS/ BENEFITS/ATTRIBUTES THAT:
(A) SEPARATE BRANDS
(B) LEAD TO PREFERENCE

PHASE 2

DEFINE & DESCRIBE MARKET IN TERMS OF:

CONCEPTUAL IMAGE OF OURS AND COMPETITIVE BRANDS

DEMOGRAPHY, SOCIO-ECONOMICS ATTITUDES, OPINIONS, INTERESTS LIFESTYLES OF PRIMARY USERS. ALSO DETERMINE VOLUMES CONSUMED BY BRAND

PRIMARY USERS' WANTS/NEEDS/ DESIRES

DEVELOP BRAND MAP BASED ON CONCEPTUAL ATTRIBUTES & BRAND POSITIONINGS

FORM & DESCRIBE SEGMENTS OF SIMILAR WANTS, NEEDS & DESIRES & ESTIMATE SIZE OF EACH SEGMENT BASED ON NUMBER OF PERSONS & VOLUME OF DEMAND

DEVELOP A MAP BASED ON THE CONCEPTUAL ATTRIBUTES SHOWING THE RELATIONSHIP OF SEGMENTS AND BRANDS

ASSESS MAP TO DETERMINE MARKETING STRATEGY FOR EXISTING BRANDS AND POTENTIAL FOR DEVELOPING NEW BRANDS

PHASE 3

FOR EACH BRAND DECISION, DEFINE TARGET SEGMENT:
-DEMOGRAPHICS
-LIFESTYLE
-PERSONALITIES
-ATTITUDES TO PRODUCT CLASS
-OCCASIONS FOR USE
-CURRENT BRAND CHOICES
-GEOGRAPHIC LOCATION

SPECIFY PRODUCT TO PRODUCTION BASED ON TARGET SEGMENT'S NEEDS & WANTS

DEVELOP DETAILED SET OF COMMUNICATIONS SPECIFICATIONS FOR BRAND BASED ON TARGET SEGMENTS NEEDS AND WANTS

PHASE 4

MANUFACTURE VARIETY OF TEST PRODUCTS

CONSUMER PRODUCT TEST EXPERIMENTAL PRODUCTS WITH TARGET MARKET

DEVELOP PRICING PHILOSOPHY

DEVELOP ROUGH GRAPHIC ALTERNATIVES

DEVELOP ADVERTISING CONCEPT ALTERNATIVES

DEVELOP OTHER COMMUNICATIVE ELEMENTS:
-P.O.S.
-PROMOTIONS
-SALES KIT

CONSUMER TEST FINISHED GRAPHICS, ADVERTISING, PRICE AND OTHER COMMUNICATIVE ELEMENTS WITH TARGET GROUP

PHASE 5

QUANTITATIVELY CONSUMER TEST COMMUNICATIVE ELEMENTS AND PRODUCT TO DETERMINE:
(A) WHETHER COMMUNICATIVE ELEMENTS ARE IN CONCERT WITH EACH OTHER
(B) WHETHER COMMUNICATIVE ELEMENTS ARE IN CONCERT WITH THE PRODUCT
(C) CONSUMER ACCEPTANCE OF THE WHOLE PROPOSITION

IF NECESSARY ADJUST PRODUCT AND/OR COMMUNICATIVE ELEMENTS BASED ON PREVIOUS QUANTITATIVE CONSUMER MARKET RESEARCH

LAUNCH/RELAUNCH BRAND

PHASE 6

MONITOR BRAND'S PERFORMANCE AND COMPETITIVE ACTIVITY AT REGULAR INTERVALS ment dealers. A bank that looks for WIFMs only against other banks may discover a WIFM that makes it superior to every other bank. But there may be a credit union out there that is better on that WIFM.

Here's another example: An ad for one of the leading antiseptic skin cleansers was at the beginning of a teen magazine. In the middle of the same publication was an advertisement for a medicated pad. The medicated pad advertiser was smart enough to take into account the fact that it competes with the antiseptic skin cleanser subsegment. It built its superiority claim around the fact that it wipes out pimples, whereas not all antiseptic skin cleansers do. The advertisement even showed three antiseptic cleansers in the background to help the consumer recognize the specific, inferior brands. But the advertiser forgot something important, as illustrated in the ad for the Oxy Clean medicated pad, which appeared toward the end of the same publication.

The sequence of ads was terrific, if anyone besides me noticed. First there was an advertisement for an antiseptic skin cleanser that said, WE DEEP CLEAN. But this company forgot that one of the primary reasons people want deep cleaning is to remove or prevent blemishes (the consumer need deep cleaning fulfills, and the primary benefit of the product class). This, in turn, blinded the advertiser to the fact that it competes with medicated pads. The second advertiser capitalized on this and torpedoed the antiseptic skin cleanser's claim by pointing out that deep cleaning isn't enough. The consumer needs medication to stop pimples. In short, the second advertiser told consumers why its brand meets their needs better than the whole product class of antiseptic skin cleansers.

The second advertiser was astute enough to look over its left shoulder and position itself as superior to a competitive product class, but it made the fatal mistake of forgetting to look to the right. This allowed Oxy Clean—its direct competition—to claim superiority in a head-to-head comparison. Any consumer who was following the logic of the sequencing of the ads would, of course, buy Oxy Clean—a good WIFM ad with a strong and demonstrable superiority claim.

NOW OXY CLEAN PADS ARE 28% BIGGER TO CLEAN BETTER!

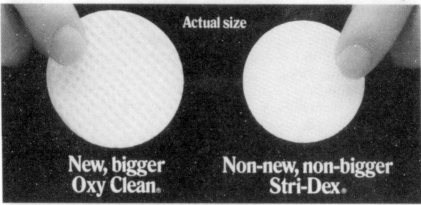

Actual size

New, bigger
Oxy Clean.

Non-new, non-bigger
Stri-Dex.

- Bigger to hold more deep-cleaning cleanser!
- Bigger to remove more dirt and oil!
- Bigger to clean better than Stri-Dex!®

TRY THEM ON FOR SIZE AND SAVE 50¢

Market Research Basics

Returning to the beer example from the beginning of the chapter, if you were a beer marketer, by now you would have a pretty good idea of the needs beer meets at the product-class level: liquid replenishment, refreshment, thirst quenching, casual relaxation. You also have some indication of the risks beer drinkers endure: addiction, bitter taste. Once you've listed needs and risks, start to think about some of the other people-type needs such as occasions for use. For example, lots of people drink beer in casual, relaxed social situations, which relates to the relaxation properties of alcohol. This scenario also gives you another clue to the needs beer meets—camaraderie or socialization. Add this to your list. Keep thinking about beer and moods or beer and life-styles. Pretty soon you will have a more complete list of the different needs beer meets at the product-class level. Then turn your attention to brand values. List how each of your competitors specifically meets each of the fourteen brand values (See Chapter 8). You now have a list of the various tactics brands use to meet product-class needs as well as add value to the product class. Within a couple of hours, you should have a list of fifty to a hundred items that will form the "guts" of your quantitative market research into the beer category. This list contains virtually every rating scale that you will use to determine consumer needs (as well as the extent to which brands are meeting these needs). This list should also tell you which one or two of the five people-type areas will be most productive for searching out needs in your category.

Every market research house has its own theory of what measurements are best suited to a particular brand, and the trick in picking a research house is not so much whether it is competent to conduct the research, but whether its theory of brand selection makes any sense and jibes with what you know about brands in your category. Steer clear of research houses that measure only people-type values and not brand values. In fact, there are many instances in which it isn't necessary to measure people needs at all. In such cases, the marketer can limit the investigation (and time and costs) to the measurement of brand values, especially when there is a strong suspicion that the competition is meeting product-class needs very well.

You should also avoid researchers that recommend asking consumers directly what influences them to select one brand over another, or asks them to rank order a series of variables from the most important to the least important in their selection of a brand. This firm does not understand the objectives of WIFM research and is ignoring a marketing reality as well as breaking a fundamental rule of market research.

First, the marketing reality that is being ignored is that in many product categories a consumer can use more than one brand in the same category at any point in time, depending on the circumstance or occasion. With the success of market segmentation, most markets have become multibrand markets. A perfect example of this is soft drinks: a consumer may prefer one brand when it is extremely hot outside and she wants to cool off quickly and another brand when she just craves a sweet taste. When occasions for use or seasonality play a role in the selection of brands, you can't ask consumers to rank order their reasons for selecting a brand. Or rather you can ask, but the answer will be meaningless because the reasons change based on the situation.

Second, asking consumers to rank order a series of selection variables breaks one of the basic rules of market research: Ask respondents only one question at a time. When you ask a multipart question, you never know which part is being answered. By asking consumers to rank a series of items in order of importance to brand selection, you are asking at least three questions—maybe more. For each brand image characteristic, you are asking the consumer to (1) assess whether the characteristic even fits the brand at all, (2) assess the amount of that characteristic the brand in question possesses, and (3) tell you whether that amount led to selection.

Asking consumers directly why they select one brand over another is not a sound research method either. Some consumers may know themselves well enough to play the researcher's game of describing the reasons behind their choices, but many buy on intuition or for sociological reasons, and they will never take the time to analyze each purchase decision the way a market researcher requires. For example, alcoholic beverages are consumed primarily in groups; therefore, the informal group leader has a strong influence on the brands of alcoholic beverages purchased by group members. Most consumers are not even aware of this, and those that are wouldn't tell you that they were influenced to buy a particular brand by someone else anyway. In other instances, consumers—who have never given much thought to brands in the way you are asking them to—gravitate toward the most logical reasons for selecting a brand and away from the emotional reasons (which could be more important). In still other instances, some consumers give the answers that seem intelligent rather than the real reasons, because they want to impress the interviewer.

Since the direct approach doesn't work, the market research firm has to get at attributes that lead to brand selection through the back door, so to speak. The researcher will have to build statistical techniques into the questionnaire and analyses that will allow differentiation between the attributes that lead to brand selection and those that do not. Through good statistical techniques, it is possible to know precisely why each respondent in the sample selects one brand over another. The right market research house will be able to explain how to do this inferentially rather than directly.

Determining the "Ideal" Brand

Because market research fieldwork is done at a single point in time, such research is merely a view of the world at that time; it does not give insight into the world of the future. But with a little extra work, consumers can also tell you how your entire industry could be changed to make it better for them.

Of course, you can't ask consumers directly how to change your industry. The market researcher's job is to be creative in pulling meaningful information from consumers, and a creative researcher does this inferentially by looking at the respondent's dream or vision of the future. I discovered this trick some time ago while trying to find out why women didn't drink beer as much as men did. One woman in a focus group said, "I wish I liked the taste of beer." Once she opened up the subject, what came tumbling out from all the respondents was their dream world—all the positive imagery associated with beer such as relaxation, informal fun in the sun, camaraderie, and beer's distinctive ability to quench thirst, *but* in a beverage that tasted good to them. This vision or dream is the "ideal brand."

Quantitatively, most market researchers obtain the ideal by having the respondent rate a hypothetical brand called the "ideal" or "perfect" brand on the same rating scales used for existing brands in the marketplace. This hypothetical ideal, when compared to the ratings for every brand in the market, gives a lot of valuable information that would not have been obtained if only existing brands had been measured. For example, if every real brand was doing a poor job on a certain characteristic that was important to the consumer, this would show up only in a comparison of existing brands to the ideal.

Perhaps Palmolive used this technique in the automatic dishwashing detergent market to determine that no one was delivering in the important area of not leaving residue on glasses. Perhaps it found that all brands delivered at a three rating on the ten-point residue scale when in fact the ideal rating was nine. Palmolive seized the opportunity by introducing a liquid automatic dishwashing detergent that eliminated the granular residue problem. A comparison of existing brands to the ideal often spawns new subsegments, as this example shows.

Miller Lite capitalized on an entire industry's failure to address the "fattening" perceptions of beer. This would not have shown up if the rating for regular beers had been used as the standard for what consumers wanted.

More often, the ideal will spawn new design or formulation criteria for an existing brand that is useful for rejuvenation purposes.

The graph in Figure 10-2 is from a presentation I gave a newspaper client on how the product could better meet the needs of existing and potential readers. In this particular study we examined sixty-five different aspects of the newspaper, including people-type needs, product-class risks such as the balance between bad news and good news, plus specific brand values that covered the various functional areas of a newspaper (e.g., circulation, advertising, editorial). This graph shows just some of the items we measured to determine whether the

Figure 10-2. Ideal vs. actual needs satisfaction.

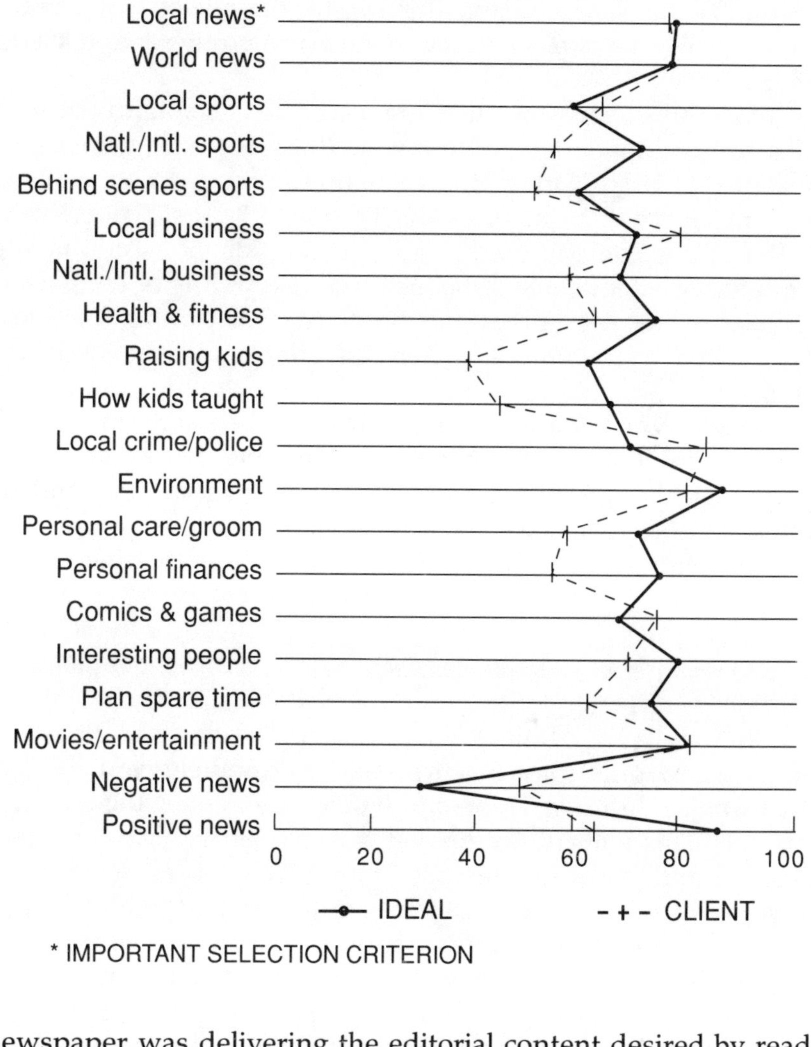

newspaper was delivering the editorial content desired by readers. Note that the client was meeting expectations (the "ideal" line) in many editorial areas, but was deficient in the amount of news requested by readers in the areas of national and international sports, national and international business, health and fitness, raising kids, how kids are taught, personal care and grooming, personal finances, and how to plan spare time. It was also delivering too much bad news and not enough good news.

Overall, however, the editorial group was doing a terrific job of meeting readers' needs, and this is why the newspaper continues to grow despite stiff competition from other papers and other media.

No matter how the data are used, it is foolhardy not to collect ideal brand data. Without it, there is no benchmark to measure against, other than competitors. And without a benchmark, you might erroneously conclude that, collectively, all the brands on the market are meeting all the needs in the marketplace adequately. Obviously the research is only as good as the variables measured, but the point is that unless the ideal is measured, you won't see where the entire industry is missing the boat.

To take the "ideal" one step further and expand on Phase 2 of the model, it should be pointed out that market segments can be defined by grouping people with homogeneous (similar) wants and needs. In well-executed research, this grouping is done on the ideal brand ratings rather than existing brand ratings.

Quantitative-Qualitative Research

Although I recommend quantitative research at Phase 2, budgets and time may preclude this. Fortunately, you can get much the same information through well-executed focus group research. This will cut the market research budget by 75 percent or more and collapse the time frame even more. You *cannot*, however, do normal types of focus group research. What is required is quantitative measures using qualitative techniques, and that is a special skill that few group moderators can do well.

The moderator must use focus group techniques to arrive at brand ratings for the key benefits of the brand and product class. I usually use models of the brands themselves and have the group, as a whole, move the models around on a key rating dimension one at a time, so that we get the rank order of the brands on that dimension. In another case, I had the group tell me the things that made the best brands on the market best for them. Then we talked about how these brands could be improved. This gave us the ideal rating, but it also pointed out where each of the existing brands stood relative to the ideal.

Although it sounds easy to do qualitatively, be careful. The biggest problem with groups is that respondents are not recruited randomly; therefore, the results may not be projectable to the population at large. There are two ways around this problem: Either recruit the groups at random or keep doing groups until the answers start to form an unbreakable pattern. Both work well, and although they drive up the cost and time benefits of groups, these options are still cheaper and less time-consuming than doing a large quantitative study.

Phase 3: Brand Positioning

Phase 3 of the model is the most critical part of the exercise. At this point you know your brand's current position in the consumer's mind and where the market opportunities are. The question is: How much does your brand have to change to be more successful in the market? You have the data to answer this question. You have the ratings of your own and competitive brands; you can see where you need to pull up your socks, and you know each competitor's Achilles' heel. More than that, you have clusters or segments of real live consumers who have similar wants and needs. And since the segments were created by grouping those who wanted the same things in their ideal brand, you can see by the volume consumed by each segment (or group of wants and needs) which are the volume opportunities and which are the niche segments.

The output at Phase 2 forms the main ingredient for assessment at Phase 3. If you have a good handle on the marketplace through either good grass-roots communication with consumers or good marketing intelligence, the output at Phase 2 shouldn't have yielded too many surprises. The data most likely confirmed your judgment and will merely assist in refining the existing brand positioning. If nothing else, such research forces you to review and, if necessary, refine or readjust the elements in the brand's marketing mix. This is a worthwhile task at any time in a brand's life, but it is especially useful when you have fresh positioning research that objectively shows where every brand in the marketplace sits, relative to what consumers really want.

A competent research house will be able to develop a "map" of the Phase 2 output showing the key brand selection criteria as axes on the map. Placed on this grid are brands and segments, resulting in a clear, concise picture of the market as it now exists and as the consumer wishes it to be. If the research house is experienced, it will not develop a map with more than two dimensions. There are lots of techniques for displaying more than two dimensions, but my experience has been that the mainstream of any market can be described quite well by focusing on the two main items that led to the consumers' selection of a brand. Any more than two dimensions confuses the client company, if not the researcher. The map has to communicate so clearly that the position for the client's brand jumps off the page. To clutter up the map with a lot of esoteric information (just because the data were gathered) doesn't do anyone a service. If more than two dimensions are needed to describe the market, this can be accomplished in a series of maps.

A typical positioning map in the laundry detergent market would start out looking like this:

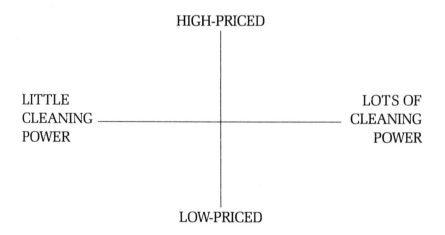

The two axes of price and cleaning power represent the two main reasons consumers select one brand of laundry detergent over another. We could have muddied the map by adding liquid versus powder or those brands that have fabric softener in them, but these subsegments and other reasons for selection are easily handled on a second or third map.

There are some powerful statistical software packages that group people together based on their wants and needs. First the computer cuts the sample into two pieces based on the most important selection criterion—cleaning power. The cuts the computer makes are illustrated in a tree diagram (Figure 10-3). This first cut results in two segments—those who want a lot of cleaning power (85 percent), and those who are less concerned about cleaning power (15 percent). The computer then takes these two groups of people and cuts them on the price they are prepared to pay for the ideal detergent, resulting in four segments.

Figure 10-3. Tree diagram.

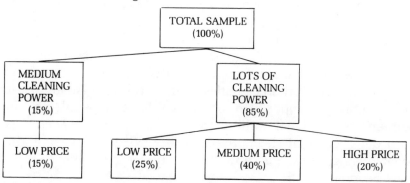

At this point, the reason for the 15 percent segment wanting less cleaning power in a brand of detergent starts to emerge: They don't want to pay a whole lot of money for the detergent, so they cannot reasonably ask for a lot of cleaning power. In all likelihood, they cannot afford more expensive detergent, so they buy strictly on price. This is where the art of market segmentation starts to emerge. The only difference between this low-price segment and the other low-price segment (25 percent) is the amount of cleaning power desired. The question then arises: Are they really different segments, or are these just statistical observations? This question can usually be answered through a series of investigations:

- Are the two groups very different demographically or geographically?
- Do the same brands appeal to both segments?
- Does the 25 percent segment exist only because it believes that all brands have the same cleaning power, meaning that the choice is based strictly on price (the generic brand buyer)?
- If the computer were to make another cut, would a third important reason for selection emerge for either segment?

If the investigation shows real and substantial differences between the two segments, keep them separated; otherwise collapse them into one large segment. Perhaps the low-priced/medium cleaning power group buys only nationally advertised brands, whereas the low-priced/lots of cleaning power group usually buys store brands or generics. Such a finding would suggest leaving them as separate segments.

The 40 percent medium-priced/lots of cleaning power segment is the heart of the market. Usually the leading brand and all its "me-too" imitators appeal to this segment. The demographic and other characteristics of this segment usually depict the "average shopper." In other words, the people in this segment usually have nothing more in common than their need for a detergent that cleans the best (the WIFM). This shouldn't be surprising, since we know that needs are more homogenous than people.

The 20 percent high-priced segment is the so-called premium segment. These people usually believe that one detergent cleans better than all the rest, and they are willing to pay a premium for this difference. Although this segment may contain upscale people, it probably doesn't in this market. It more likely contains consumers with special cleaning needs (lots of young kids, husband is a mechanic, and so on) for whom cleaning power is everything.

Now that we've described the segments and understand a little about the needs of the detergent market, it is time to add these four segments to our "map" (Figure 10-4). (In reality, this is a very simplistic map. In highly competitive markets like the detergent market, there are probably ten to twenty segments of

Figure 10-4. Filled-in positioning map.

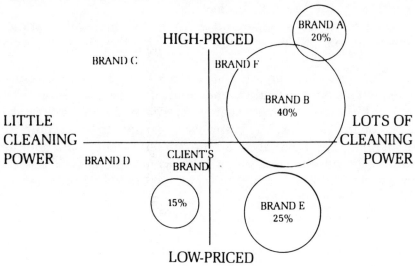

homogeneous needs. I have simplified it just to get the idea across.) Each of the four segments is shown as a circle, and the size of the circle represents the size of the segment. I usually show size in terms of volume of product consumed rather than numbers of people, because the strategic issue for the marketer is to sell as much volume as possible. I also put the current image of the main brands in the market on the map. Now it really starts to tell a story.

Clearly, Brand A is well positioned against the premium segment. By checking Brand A's image against the ideal brand rating of consumers in the 20 percent segment, you can look for areas of deficiency. Since the brand is pretty close to the center of the segment, however, you are not likely to find major problems that you can exploit.

The same holds true for Brand B. It occupies a space right in the center of the 40 percent segment. This makes it the market leader, and if you compare its image to the ideal of the segment, you will see that it has few exploitable problems. There is little opportunity to move the leader from the top spot until the market shifts or Brand B gets sloppy and either stops delivering what the 40 percent segment wants or delivers less of what is expected by the heart of the market.

The same goes for Brand E. It is the high-value brand, delivering lots of cleaning power at low prices (high quality x low price = value).

There are three brands that are not close to any segment—the client's brand, Brand C, and Brand D. The client's brand is reasonably close to three segments, but it doesn't satisfy the needs of any of them. The brand was designed to be all things to all people, but there it is at the center of the map offering nothing to no one. The client is in trouble because it doesn't have a clear WIFM in a highly segmented market dominated by strong WIFM brands.

So what are the options? It would be preferable to compete in the larger segments, but Brands A, B, and E clearly cover these segments well. There is only one option: Lower the price and compete directly against the 15 percent segment. Since the research revealed that this segment prefers to buy nationally advertised brands, the client will have to promote the new low price extensively.

Because the client's brand is already perceived as mid-range on cleaning power, a lower price makes it an excellent value for the 15 percent segment, so this is likely to be the WIFM—value. The client can't claim, however, that its brand cleans as well as Brand B or Brand E, because the market doesn't believe that. It can, however, claim to clean better than Brands C and D (now both higher-priced brands). This will establish the value claim based on current perceptions in the marketplace. This WIFM is, therefore, demonstrable and believable.

With some extra work, this marketer should have little difficulty establishing the client's brand in the 15 percent segment. However, the client will likely resist this positioning initially, because it's the smallest segment, which puts a ceiling on ability to grow. It's also the lowest margin segment because of the demand for national advertising, so the marginal profit per unit will be smaller. But when it all washes out, a dominant share of a small segment, even at lower margins, will net much more bottom-line profit than the client is currently getting from the larger segments.

Phase 4: Conforming Tactics and Positioning

Phase 4 is primarily for new product development work, so you may or may not want to use all the elements. In our laundry detergent example, if the profit margin can't be improved by cheapening the product without lowering its actual cleaning power, the client may skip the entire left-hand side of Phase 4.

Because the new target group buys nationally advertised brands, however, the detergent marketer will definitely have to use the communications side of Phase 4. This will take some time and quite a bit of money to do correctly. Market research should be used to test the various elements of the revised position, *but only among target group consumers*—the ones in the 15 percent segment. Any competent research house should be able to select these people based on rating scales or brands purchased now that the initial research has been done.

Focus group research is most often used in Phase 4. Although the research objective is to screen alternatives (alternative package designs, alternative advertising, and alternative promotional schemes), which implies quantification, I have found it most useful to again combine qualitative and quantitative research in focus groups at this stage. To do this, I usually show the focus group the series of alternatives (three ads, for example) and then have them rate their preferences and impressions on some type of rating scales. The group members cannot talk, groan, or use body language, nor can they look at what their fellow group members are writing. This minimizes the social effects of groups, since at this stage you want individual, not collective, judgments. Once the ratings have been obtained, we discuss why they liked or disliked the alternatives, as well as why the ads gave different impressions about the WIFM we were attempting to communicate. Depending on the subject matter, this can be fruitful for obtaining in-depth feelings, since you automatically establish groups that are pro or con a particular alternative or perception.

You can also quickly see if a particular ad is delivering more than one message. This is a no-no in WIFM advertising, since the name of the game is to tell consumers, in the simplest and most direct way possible, why your brand is so superior to the competition that they should buy it. In our detergent example, we want to communicate good value (low price and medium cleaning power). If the target group is getting a second or different message, *no matter how much we and the agency like the ad*, it should not be used because it does not clearly and concisely communicate the WIFM.

The one part of Phase 4 that should not be tested in focus groups is pricing. Testing pricing alternatives in focus groups usually results in poor or sometimes misleading answers because of people's reluctance to reveal their financial status. In our detergent example, where we are aiming at people who want the lowest price possible, it may be difficult for people to tell other members of the group that they are so poor that they can't afford anything more expensive. It is therefore best to use quantitative research techniques to test the price elasticity issue.

Phase 5: Researching All the Elements Together

Phase 5 is a critical part of the process, yet most marketers have spent so much time and expense in the preceding phases that they often skip Phase 5 because they are champing at the bit to launch and see if they did it right. This can be a risky decision because up to now, each element of the brand has been worked on independently. For example, the work on the product has been separate from the work on the brand's image. And in some cases the image conveyed by the package has been examined in isolation from the image carried by the advertising. Phase 5 brings all the pieces together under one research umbrella to determine whether they are all in sync. To me, building a brand is like building any structure. If any major element is weak or not in sync with the other pieces, the entire structure could collapse. That's what Phase 5 determines.

Market research work at this stage should isolate the major elements of the brand and determine the extent to which they contribute to the overall success (or potential failure) of the brand and the degree to which the elements complement one another. This work can be very revealing if done correctly. One of my clients recently discovered that the product was contributing to the potential success of the brand significantly more than the imagery elements of the brand (package, label, and advertising). This directed the marketers to refine the imagery elements to better express the real and perceived product characteristics so that all the elements worked toward the common expression of the brand's WIFM. The result was a much stronger presentation to the consumer that generated significantly higher intent-to-purchase scores when the Phase 5 market research was redone. And since the product was such a strong piece of the puzzle, this alerted the marketers to an opportunity to gain significant trial and repeat purchases through the effective use of sampling.

Phase 6: Tracking Results

Phase 6 is the tracking phase. Here you determine whether the message is getting through to the right people and resulting in brand switching. Part of the monitoring should be devoted to tracking the images of other brands as well, since although they are doing a good job of satisfying consumer needs today, they may slip up. You want to be ready to jump in with just the right combination of product and image in order to fill the void. Successful companies develop brands for the other segments and keep them on the shelf until the timing is just right.

We were even able to build a simplified version of the ideal brand idea into one client's tracking studies. This allowed him to see whether the entire market was shifting in a certain direction and he could monitor wholesale changes, without doing expensive market segmentation studies every few years. We continue to track two major trends that started in the 1970s and still have a massive effect on almost every market: the concern for physical well-being and the search for value.

The concern for well-being spawned the light/lite craze and has recently shown up as a determined search for less fat. It has also resulted in a concern about chemicals used in products, overpackaging, and manufacturing processes. There is little doubt that the concern for individual welfare has grown into a much more global concern—the concern for our species and planet as expressed in environmental issues.

The value issue has resulted in major segmentation on the price-quality variables in almost all product classes. Many marketers learned the difference between high price and high value in the 1980s: The consumer rejects high-priced, low-quality brands because the product does not live up to its value claim.

Nobody knows where these trends come from. Some are biologically induced (as Yuppies get older, they are more concerned about their health), some are environmental (by just looking around us we can see the degree to which we are destroying our environment through waste, misuse, and pollution), and some are sociological (self-indulgence has lost its appeal for those who have discovered that "toys" can't buy happiness).

No matter where they come from, it is necessary to monitor the broader trends that are going on in society to see the extent to which they will affect your particular market.

The Six WIFM Positioning Stances

There are at least nineteen potential needs that can be fulfilled: the five people needs and the fourteen brand value needs. Your brand's ability to fulfill one of these needs better than the competition (if you have any) will be the WIFM for the brand.

Once you have found the WIFM, however, it is necessary to tell consumers what your brand stands for so they will be sure to put it in the right need-fulfillment slot. There are six stands you can take to give yourself strategic superiority, depending on your position in the marketplace.

Take a Stand

Position in Marketplace	*Stand*
Monopoly/industry association/brand leader	1. Leadership 2. Risk reduction
One brand among many	3. Marketing warfare 4. New category 5. Market expansion 6. Niche

1. *Leadership Stance.* Position the brand as superior to all other brands in the category (or as superior to other product classes) in doing what the product class was supposed to do in the first place. If you are not the leader in a category that has no direct competition from other categories, an industry association intent on increasing primary demand, or a monopoly, you should not even attempt this positioning.

2. *Risk-Reduction Stance.* Position the brand as reducing the risk inherent in using the product class. This positioning stance usually results in the creation of a new subsegment of the parent product class.

3. *Marketing-Warfare Stance.* When you find that the brand leader no longer fulfills the consumer needs the product class was designed to fulfill, position the brand against the major product-class need. This is a variation on the leadership stance in which you challenge the existing leader in the category. Make sure you have deep pockets, lots of patience, and an incredible amount of courage when you take this positioning stance, however. And also make sure that you are right about the leader having an exploitable vulnerability. To be wrong when you challenge the leader usually results in death.

4. *New-Category Stance.* Position the brand as changing most or all of the benefits of the product class as previously defined. Since you have essentially wiped out the product class as consumers once knew it, you have made the competition obsolete. This is hard to achieve, but well worth the effort. Once you have made the competition obsolete, you have essentially given yourself a monopoly position until someone enters the new category you have created.

5. *Market-Expansion Stance.* Position the brand to appeal to a larger group of needs that have been uncovered in contiguous product classes. Here the marketer looks at the needs in contiguous product classes and designs the brand to fulfill needs in two or more classes simultaneously. Two-in-one shampoo-conditioners are a current example of this positioning technique, as are banks that sell life and health insurance.

6. *Niche Stance.* Position the brand as a subsegment of the product class based on a more targeted or narrower interpreta-

tion of the original needs that were being met by the product class. Our detergent example did this, and this is where most brands will wind up when following the WIFM positioning exercise. Here the marketer positions the brand as superior to the competition in meeting one of the fourteen brand-value needs.

One of these six will be your WIFM brand-positioning stance.

11

The Care and Feeding of WIFMs

Now that you have arrived at a WIFM brand positioning that answers the consumers' superiority question, there are a few rules of thumb to take into account before you cast the position in stone and announce your positioning stance to consumers.

The Basics of WIFM Positioning

Rule 1: Demonstrability

It might seem trite to say that a WIFM has to be demonstrable, but some marketers still don't understand how important this is.

Clones

There are so many brands that are merely clones of successful brands that the marketing industry has given them a name—"me-too" brands.

Hundreds of me-too brands are spun out each year as a result of the short-term, reactive thinking that seems to pervade most North American marketing environments. In some instances the marketer lacks creativity and opts to take the easy way out by copying a successful competitor. In other cases, the marketer forgets to distinguish between brands and product classes, leading to the belief that a new brand must look a lot like others in the category to make consumers "feel comfortable" with the brand.

Such thinking is based on a lack of understanding of the intelligence of consumers and the proven fact that consumers will change their buying patterns if they find something new and different that better meets their needs. Further, this type of thinking leads marketers away from the central fact that brands have to demonstrate at least a difference to be noticed. WIFMs take this one step further by saying that difference is not enough. Superiority over other brands in the product class is the central issue for marketers intent on product-class domination. Wear-Dated carpets demonstrate a superior difference from their competitors in the pictured ad, and this is what makes them the hot consumer item they are today.

In some cases, marketers use cloning when they need to react quickly. When Palmolive put out a liquid dishwashing detergent and caught its competitors sleeping, the quickest course of action for the competition to stem the market-share erosion was to create a me-too of Palmolive. And that's exactly what they did. But because the didn't offer the consumer anything better, they were relegated to a humiliating second- and third-place status in market share, and will likely remain there for a long time.

There is one instance, however, in which cloning can result in market dominance: when the market leader has been caught sleeping by a young upstart *with no proven track record* that introduces an entirely new subproduct class. If the market leader, which has a history of product excellence in the category, clones the upstart's invention, the market leader often emerges the winner. Why? Because the market leader can give the consumer both the new invention and a value-added brand WIFM (or corporate WIFM, in some instances) of proven quality over a long period of time. This cannot be duplicated by the young upstart, so unless it can make a further improvement on the original invention, it is likely to lose the dominant position.

This happened to Wilkinson Sword when it introduced the first twin-blade shaving cartridge. The market leader, Gillette,

Very funny, Mrs. Lenzen.

You had to do it, didn't you, Mrs. Lenzen.
You couldn't be like the 250,000 other people who finally gave up trying to stain their free sample of Wear-Dated® Carpet with StainBlocker.™ Well, you got us. Wear-Dated Carpet does not prevent holes caused by battery acid. But thanks to people all across America who tested our carpet against *their* toughest stains, we can now say Wear-Dated Carpet with StainBlocker offers stain protection never before available. And thanks to you, Mrs. Lenzen, we also have to suggest that everyone keep their car off the carpet. For now.

WEAR-DATED CARPET
WITH STAINBLOCKER™

had concentrated on safety blades and had missed this techni-
cally superior shaving innovation and lost a lot of business to
Wilkinson. When Gillette finally introduced a twin-blade cartridge, it regained consumer loyalty because it offered the same
product as Wilkinson, but with the Gillette name on it. Gillette
has since made several other technology-driven improvements
to the original cartridge, which has further cemented its dominance of the market. But just because Gillette did it doesn't
mean that everyone can. Only in those instances where the
market leader has been so dominant in the category for a very
long time will cloning likely result in regaining the dominant
position, especially if the cloned brand does not retaliate.

IBM is another example. Over the years, IBM has let Apple
and Compaque and a host of other brands introduce innovation
after innovation. But when IBM finally gets around to introducing its own version, it quickly captures massive market share.
One has to wonder, however, how long consumers will put up
with the market leader being a follower. IBM was late with the
PC, late with the portable, and late with the computer notebook.
Perhaps IBM's recent problems stem from not playing a leadership role in a market it has dominated for so long.

In all but the exceptional cases noted, it is better to resist the
urge to clone; bide your time and make the second entry in the
category better than the first. Although marketing statistics often
show that the first brand in a category dominates the category
for years, this is not necessarily true when a second or third
entry meets consumer needs better. The truth is, in many cases,
clones can help make the first brand dominant for years.

In his book *Winning at New Products,* Dr. Robert Cooper
reports the results of his study of the reasons for the success or
failure of over 3,500 new products. The number-one reason for
failure is that most new products aren't new—they are merely
clones of an existing brand that do not offer the consumer any
product advantage. To quote Cooper: "The most important single new product success factor was having a superior new
product that delivered significant and unique benefits to the end
user." Cooper found that "the odds of success with a superior
and unique product were over 89 percent. In contrast, the
'me-too' or 'ho-hum' products achieved a success rate of only 28

percent. In other words, superior and unique products were three times more likely to succeed than me-too products."

"First is best" works only if first is absolutely right for the consumer. Most first-is-best marketers are short-term thinkers who employ a brand-positioning technique called tracking the competition, not tracking the consumer. Perhaps they have lost sight of the fact that their brands are designed to meet the needs of consumers. And meeting consumer needs is a long-term issue that only consumers can help them with.

Some companies have a new-product strategy of "launch first and fix later." These companies believe that being first in a new category or subclass guarantees market-share dominance. Such a philosophy, however, almost guarantees failure if the competition is strong and launches a second or third brand that meets consumer needs better. The "launch first and fix later" company won't have time to fix it if there is strong competition.

"Owning" a WIFM

Another aspect of the need to demonstrate the WIFM in the actual product is the myth among a handful of marketers that if you say something long enough and loud enough, consumers will eventually believe it, whether the brand delivers it or not. This has been proved untrue over and over.

One coffee brand stands out as a particularly good example of this. It has said with a lot of media weight and for a long time that its brand is the richest tasting coffee in the world. On the surface, this seems to be a WIFM because it is a sensory superiority statement. But the brand that makes this superiority claim breaks three fundamental WIFM rules simultaneously: (1) with almost all brands of coffee claiming to be the richest tasting, this brand gets lost in the general noise; (2) *rich tasting* is one of those unfortunate advertising terms that has several meanings, which makes it a poor WIFM term when you are trying to tell consumers precisely and specifically why they should buy your brand over the competition; and (3) this brand makes no attempt to prove that it is the richest coffee in the world.

Brand strategists often refer to an opportunity to "own a particular benefit." Most often this opportunity is based on a thorough evaluation of the advertising strategies of the competition and the discovery that one of the product-class variables remains unclaimed by any competitor in its advertising. The advice to try to own this benefit is bad advice. If it's a product-class need, it is likely that yours and every other brand in the product class is meeting that need. You can be assured that no matter how long and hard you shout it in your advertising, you cannot own it because consumers already believe it about your brand *and the competition*. WIFM brand positioning is all about "owning" a space in the consumer's head. But you can't own a space occupied by several other brands or product categories.

Sensory Superiority

The WIFM for many brands lies in the area of sensory superiority—tastes best, smells best, looks best, feels best, or sounds best—yet this is the one area that is probably the least communicated in marketing. Many brands currently using Badge Theory or life-style advertising would probably like to come out and tell consumers that their brands' good looks are the reason they sell so well. But only a handful of brands have told consumers about their appealing designs. Honda did so in the tasteful ad pictured by using a direct approach to say why Hondas are superior in design—they don't copy everyone else. Jaguar did so by using the Jaguar brand personality to metaphorically represent its sleek, classic, powerful-looking designs.
Superiority that can be seen, tasted, felt, smelled, or heard is an area that is still untapped from a creative perspective. It is pretty discouraging to look through a leading women's magazine and count the number of perfume ads that advertise essentially the same way. This is formula advertising, not WIFM advertising.

The Five Formulas Everyone Uses

1. Just show a "beauty shot" of the perfume bottle.
2. Show a glamorous woman who is supposed to be wearing the perfume in a glamorous setting.

3. Show a sexy guy who is supposed to get turned on by the perfume.
4. Associate the brand with some exciting life-style group in the hopes that potential purchasers will want to wear the brand like a badge to identify themselves with that group. Mini-dramas featuring the perfume-wearer performing James Bond antics are the current manifestation of this formula.
5. Associate the brand with a famous personality.

When you are in the business of offering only taste or smell or visual appeal, it is extremely difficult to get a superiority message across. It is very difficult to achieve superiority in one of these areas, let alone talk about it. But as the old saying goes, if you've got it flaunt it. Many will argue that taste is a very personal thing that just cannot be communicated. However, in most product classes, one brand stands out as superior tasting, sounding, feeling, looking, or smelling. If you are in the business of appealing to one of the five senses and your brand is the leader in sensory appeal, this should always be your WIFM, and your advertising agency should be directed to find a way to communicate this.

Ads like the one from Honda show that the advertising community can respond to the challenge of finding new and creative approaches to the problems of communicating sensory superiority. In doing so, they also serve the consumer by moving the advertising industry away from product-class, Badge Theory advertising that shows pretty pictures with brands attached to them—a creative style that does little more than tell people that the brand exists.

Rule 2: Nonreproducibility

Look for a WIFM that can't be easily copied or that costs too much to duplicate. The toothpaste pump dispenser was not one of these. Colgate probably enjoyed some short-term share gains, but when Crest and everyone else copied the move a short time later, consumers had to make a brand choice on other criteria

(Text continued on page 164.)

There is one design we've

The cookie cutter. It's one tool Honda engineers have never used.

Stubbornly, they continue to rely on computers, wind tunnels and test tracks as well as their own clever ideas. Perhaps this explains why the Civic DX is not just another stamped-out, look-alike hatchback.

Instead, it has a clean, distinctive shape. A long roofline. A low hoodline. It is an advanced design that can only be described as very tasty.

On the inside, it seems as if there is more room than possible, a true engineering feat. There's generous headroom, front and back. Plenty of legroom, too. All four seats slide back and recline. So there's even room to stretch out.

The Civic DX also comes with a substantial list

approach to car never taken.

of standard goodies. But then, Honda engineers would consider anything less to be, well, half-baked.

There's an adjustable steering column. Adjustable headrests. A rear window wiper/washer. A 5-speed manual shift. Front-wheel drive. And under the hood is a snappy 1.5 liter 12-valve engine. Altogether, the Civic DX has more to offer than most hatchback cars.

That's just the way the cookie crumbles.

HONDA
Civic DX Hatchback

once again. And Colgate's short-term volume gain could easily be offset by the long-term cost of moving everyone to a more expensive container (not to mention lowering the profit margin for the whole industry).

The airline industry's frequent-flier plans also come to mind in this context. Like coupons and other short-term volume generators, frequent-flier plans essentially give the product away for free as a reward for using the service on a more frequent basis. This tactic is often used in industries in which the marketer believes there is no real tangible benefit to consumers in selecting one brand over another.

I suspect that when frequent-flier plans were first initiated they were intended to be short-term, value-added, brand initiatives to generate volume just like coupons. However, much to the whole industry's chagrin, every large airline copied this initiative, and frequent-flier programs became not a WIFM but a new price-of-entry benefit consumers now expect from every brand in the product class. I don't envy the first airline that suspends its frequent-flier program.

There are two related issues that the airline that started all this never thought of. First, the cost of these programs is enormous, and it comes straight off the bottom line. Not only do airlines give away their services for free, they have the added costs of marketing the programs on top of marketing the airlines themselves.

Second, and more important, is that the airline that started this in Canada had such a superior image that it didn't need any additional value-added brand variable to market itself. Market research conducted at the time showed that consumers would use this airline even if it did not offer a frequent-flier plan because they have had so many bad experiences with its principal competition over the years. The airline had such a clear-cut WIFM that consumers' selection decisions were uninfluenced by this costly new program. That doesn't mean that consumers aren't grateful for the program—they are—but who wouldn't appreciate being handed several thousands of dollars worth of free travel for doing what they were going to do anyway?

The point is to make sure that your WIFM is truly yours and can't be easily copied or appropriated by the competition.

Rule 3: Appealing to the Heart of the Market

Every market consists of many pockets of consumers with differing wants and needs that no one brand can possibly fulfill completely. But consumers and manufacturers cannot enjoy the benefits of mass production and mass merchandising if consumers have their own tailor-made versions of every product. So for sound reasons, products are designed to deliver benefits that cover the largest number of people possible.

For most marketers, the issue is moving volume, and the volume is at the center, or heart, of the market. The reason for this is simple: In every market, there is one primary consumer need that a large percentage of consumers have. The brand that claims to meet this consumer need best and consistently delivers this WIFM will be the market leader. However, the market starts to segment into smaller pockets of demand once secondary or tertiary desires are taken into account as our detergent model showed (see Figure 10-3). Once the marketer starts to move off center and appeal to smaller groups of consumers, he puts a ceiling on his volume. However, he has little choice but to appeal to smaller, more specialized segments *if he cannot deliver the primary demand item demonstrably better than the market leader.*

If your goal is market dominance, you start your consideration of WIFMs with the primary WIFM. Ask yourself: Can my brand do the one thing that this product class was designed to do better than the market leader? Perhaps there is something in the design or formulation that can be improved to make the brand more desirable than and superior to the brand leader. If not, you then address the second-largest pocket of demand and go through the same exercise.

The argument that says Why play the segmentation game and restrict yourself to certain pockets of demand? is very appealing. But trying to be all things to all people is essentially being nothing to no one in highly segmented and competitive markets.

Even worse is not claiming to be anything. Some argue that a manufacturer should just tell consumers that its brand is available and let the consumers discover for themselves the benefits of the brand. With this strategy the manufacturer doesn't commit itself to one position and therefore run the risk of appealing to a narrow pocket of the population. Although this argument has a certain appeal, it lacks logic and makes the false assumption that consumers will take the time to notice your brand, let alone try it. Unless consumers have lots of time on their hands or are dissatisfied with every brand in the category, there is little chance that the discovery process will happen. If you took the time to develop something better, why not tell people about it? If its demonstrable superiority is close to the heart of the market, you could become the market leader faster by telling people about your WIFM. And if your superiority claim is on the fringes of the market and has a more narrow appeal, consumers will ultimately find this out and put you in a narrow niche anyway; so why try to cover it up?

As you may have gathered from the foregoing, it's easier to find WIFMs with narrow appeal than ones that "grab" a majority of consumers. But as an example of why the rule about trying to find a WIFM near the heart of the market is so important, let's look at the various strategies Chrysler and Ford employed following the successful invasion of the Japanese into the North American market. Chrysler was first off the mark and enjoyed huge success downsizing its product line completely to meet the Japanese head-on. Lee Iacocca turned a failing company around by producing vehicles that appealed to smaller niches of the population and cut into the import competition on their own turf. That was very impressive, and it certainly fits the old adage that the best defense is a good offense. Chrysler is aware, however, that it still does not compete effectively among average run-of-the-mill car buyers, who usually buy Ford or GM. This is the center of the market, where WIFMs are harder to find due to the tremendously strong competition. It will be interesting to see whether Chrysler's recent introduction of models aimed at "centroid" customers will be successful.

The company that finds WIFMs at the heart of the market reaps the big rewards, as Ford found out with its Taurus. This brand is aimed at the average, everyday car buyer and captures the primary benefit sought by consumers at the heart of the market: styling in a family sedan. (I was a little surprised to discover that the Taurus was one of the first models to go through a rigorous program of consumer market research. With the lead times and capital investments auto manufacturers deal with, I would have thought that every car brand would go through extensive consumer scrutiny before it hit the streets.) It is clear that the people at Ford listened to the customer at the heart of the market and designed and redesigned until they got it right. They even claim to have made the Taurus bigger than they originally intended, because consumers at the heart of the market have to transport 2 adults plus 2.2 kids plus the dog, cat, and groceries. The Taurus's success makes the point about the dividends at the heart of the market, as well as another point: Consumers are intelligent, and they will help you design better products if you give them a chance. The success of the Taurus also proves that consumers at the heart of the North American car market are more style conscious than the car manufacturers had been giving them credit for. In fact, when the Taurus was first launched in December 1985, many industry experts predicted that the brand would be a "turkey," just in time for Christmas.

The Japanese have chipped away at the outside of the core of the market for so long that they have finally reached the heart. Japanese cars are getting larger as they tackle the mid-size market. They might even move into the full-size market some-day, now that we no longer have a fuel crisis and big is beautiful once again. As they incorporate many of the features that have won them massive market share in the luxury segments, into more affordable, heart-of-the-market models, their share of cen-troid customers will no doubt increase.

Rule 4: One WIFM at a Time

For most, finding more than one WIFM is an unheard of luxury. But even if your competition is so bad that you can claim superiority on more than one WIFM, you should resist the temptation, for good and logical reasons.

Even if your market research indicates that your brand beats the competition in the top three brand-selection criteria, you should use only the number-one criterion as your WIFM. This is what Tide, IBM, Xerox, Crest, and all the other brand leaders have done for years, and for good reason. By using the primary brand-selection criterion, you appeal to the largest number of people, and by appealing to the largest number of people, you will sell the largest volume. Choosing to position yourself on the top three selection criteria because you think that you can appeal to more people that way is a mistake.

As other selection criteria are added to the primary one, market segmentation starts to occur, and the pie starts to be cut into smaller pieces, as we saw in Chapter 10 with the detergent example. Positioning yourself on low price and high cleaning power appeals to a smaller group than a brand positioned on high cleaning power alone. The heart of the market is prepared to pay a fair and competitive price for delivery of the main benefit of the product class. And all brands are assumed to be fairly and competitively priced and of good value—until price is mentioned. Then the consumer's antenna is raised and a whole new series of questions unfolds about why the marketer chose to make price an issue: Is this brand really cheaper than the others? Why is it cheaper? Did it cut corners to make itself cheaper? And so on.

In effect, you have made the consumer's decision to purchase more difficult, not easier as you had originally intended. And the likelihood of brand switching is greater because of the confusion that results from your mention of the second variable. Adding just one extra variable forces the consumer's mind to think in segmentation terms. In addition, if consumers are interested in lower price and high cleaning power, they now have to assess this new information about your brand against other brands in the low price, high cleaning power segment rather than against brands in the high cleaning power segment alone. You have really made their job difficult.

The other reason for using only one WIFM is the difficulty and high cost of getting even one message across in today's environment, where consumers are bombarded with hundreds of messages a day. The November 2, 1987, issue of *Marketing* reported that the average consumer is exposed to 560 messages a day. Of these 560, the average person looked at only 76 of them. And of these 76, only 12 were remembered. Unfortunately, 3 of the 12 were remembered negatively, so that left only 9 of the original 560 (2 percent) that delivered positive messages. I'll bet that each of these 9 had a strong WIFM and only one WIFM.

The confusion created by more than one WIFM can be illustrated by an example from the antacid market. For years, one of the leading brands has been telling consumers that it is for upset stomachs—to relieve gas and neutralize acid. I and many others who love food too much knew that the brand did an excellent job of relieving the stress we put on our stomachs. All of a sudden, the brand was being touted as an excellent source of calcium. Did that ever get my attention! I don't need calcium supplements, so my mind quickly erased this brand from the box marked "antacids" and put it in the box marked "calcium supplements." I thought to myself, the competition is really going to capitalize on this change in brand positioning by flaunting the fact that it is now the *only* one for upset stomachs. But I was wrong. Shortly thereafter, the rival brand used an ad that contained a double WIFM—claiming that it was *both* an antacid and a calcium supplement. Here I was, ready to turn my allegiance over to this rival and it didn't give me the reason I needed to do so.

I don't know whether the ingredients in antacids are a natural source of calcium, or whether calcium was added to the rival brand so it could make its double WIFM claim. All I know is that I want an antacid that does a good job of relieving my stomach. As a consumer, it's probably easier for me to switch to the third brand in the category, which still claims to be a good antacid.

An often used excuse for claiming more than one WIFM is the "value" excuse. Value is a combination of price and quality; therefore, many marketers claim that to make the value point, one has to state good price and good quality separately—as two separate WIFMs. The ad for Colonial cookies, however, brings home the difficulty of communicating high value when you separate value into its two components. The resulting confusion in communication is unfortunate for the manufacturer of this high-value brand.

I don't know how the purchaser defines quality in the cookie market. However, from the Colonial cookies ad, I gather that it has something to do with nutritional ingredients. Here we

PERFECT COOKIES
FOR PERFECT KIDS

Colonial
Chocolate
chip'n pecan
COOKIES

Perfectly delicious ... perfectly priced.

have a happy child pouring milk into a bag of cookies to establish visually that the cookies are of high quality. But the value message doesn't appear until the "perfectly priced" line at the end. The ad is disjointed because it breaks value into its components and tries to show the components visually and state them at the same time.

But the real winner, when it comes to more than one WIFM, is the ad for Close-Up tartar-control toothpaste. At various points in the ad, Close-Up claims to clean the teeth, whiten the teeth, give you fresher breath, give you healthier-looking teeth, control cavities, and get rid of ugly tartar. But is the brand believable to consumers when there are other brands and brand-line extensions that are committed to specializing in only one of these areas at a time? After all, a general practitioner sends you to a specialist because both the doctor and the patient know that the generalist doesn't have the same knowledge and experience that a specialist has. The same type of thinking goes into brand selection by consumers. There is a market niche for a brand that makes five or six claims simultaneously, but it's at the fifth or sixth level on the decision tree. And at that level the size of the segment is pretty small, thus relegating the brand to a smaller niche in the category.

Rule 5: Tying Brand Attributes to Consumer Benefits

The Enfield motorbike ad pictured ties the physical characteristics of the brand to the consumer needs that are met by the brand benefits: A certain-size motor meets the needs of quick pickup and enough power to carry two people; full chain guard meets the consumer's safety need; and so on. There is no confusion, and the brand's benefits to the consumer are clear.

Now take a look at the Continental tire ad. In this eye-catching ad, Conti takes a similar approach to Enfield's, but forgets to close the loop from benefits to needs. It assumes that consumers are smart enough to make the leap from the lab technician's "painstaking accuracy" in measuring the tread and cross section of each tire to their need for performance, durability, quality, and safety. And they are, but few consumers have the time or inclination to surmise the benefit of a brand when

(*Text continued on page 175.*)

Enfield introduces Explorer CG 50

Our features	Your benefits
3.3 B.H.P. engine at 6200 RPM.	Very quick pick up And enough power to carry two.
New Mikcarb Carburettor	Now get over 60 Kms per litre in actual city riding conditions
Foot operated gears	Easy and convenient gear shift. With three gears you ride smoothly and are assured of better mileage.
Aluminium die cast wheels	Identical to the wheels found on larger foreign bikes. They are rugged and stylish. Give longer life to tyres and eliminate wheel truing.
Large wheel base	1200 mm wheel base. Maximises riding safety. Lets you corner sharp turns easily, and ride on wet and slushy roads safely.
Telescopic Hydraulically damped front fork and swing arm rear suspension.	130 mm stroke front fork shock free riding. Takes the heaviest of rides with ease.Explorer is rock steady at 60 kmph.
High performance large brake drums	Makes Explorer CG 50 a very safe bike – safe enough for your family to trust.
Aerodynamic styling	Turns heads with its sleek looks and stylish faring.
Full Chain Guard	Adds to safety and gives longer life to Sproket and Chain.

MAAS/ENEX 87966

Explorer CG 50 from Enfield.
Everything you expect a motorcycle to be.
Explorer CG 50 captures the essence of motorcycle engineering. Power. Style. Ruggedness. Convenience.
And more. Over 60 Kms to the litre. High manouverability.

And an unbelievable four digit price tag.

≡EXPLORER≡CG50
A complete Mobike

Always use genuine Enfield spare parts

the manufacturer just tells them the product attributes, especially when there is strong competition that clearly states why its brand values meet consumer needs, as illustrated by the B. F. Goodrich ad.

I am a strong proponent of measuring product benefits when WIFM hunting. Such information is extremely useful to the product development people, especially in developing the value-added features in brand WIFMs that make one brand superior to another. Apart from making the message clearer, closing the loop from benefits to needs met truly makes the consumer buying decision easier.

Rule 6: Competing Wisely

Al Ries and Jack Trout, in their great book *Positioning*, cover this rule very effectively when they state:

> The suicidal bent of companies that go head-on against established competition is hard to understand. They know the score, yet they forge ahead anyway. . . . To win the battle for the mind, you can't compete head-on against a company that has a strong established position [WIFM]. You can go around, or under or over, but never head-on.

Think about what a WIFM is: For the market leader, it is that one key consumer need that it meets better than the competition. The brand leader does it better, and consumers know it, believe it, and buy the brand because of it. For another brand to claim to be better is just plain unbelievable, if not arrogant, yet it is done every day, despite the fact that it always results in disaster. There is no known example of a brand that has gone head-to-head with a strong brand leader with an established, solid, demonstrable WIFM and won.

The key to unseating the market leader is to find a vulnerability and exploit it. With few exceptions, market leaders get complacent, lazy, or greedy over time. Bide your time, continue to measure the competition for its ability to deliver its WIFM, and then when the competition has let its guard down and in some way walked away from its WIFM, pounce on the opportu-

(*Text continued on page 178.*)

nity. Many brands have done this with great success and have become the market leader. But they were able to capture market preeminence only because they followed the WIFM rules better than the competition.

Rule 7: Continuity of Elements

Although it may be difficult to do practically, the brand's name; package shape, size, and configuration; packaging graphics; and promotion and advertising should consistently state the brand's WIFM. The ad for Cutex's Every Lash Longer mascara demonstrates in the visual, the headline, and the name of the brand what makes this brand superior to the competition. All the elements of Every Lash Longer mascara are nicely integrated to state the reason consumers should buy this brand over every other brand in the marketplace: It will make your eyelashes look longer (and therefore, more appealing).

Although I believe strongly that every element of a brand should work toward its WIFM, in the real world of business you are up against enormous pressures *not* to do this. One of the strongest pressures is the one that demands that you continually increase the brand's contribution to the bottom line. If the financial vice president can show that a new package design (that is, a nonstandard, more expensive design) will cause even a short-term deterioration in bottom-line profits, the marketing vice president's argument that without this WIFM-centered package the brand's volume will be significantly smaller because its image will deteriorate over the long term will fall on deaf ears.

Fortunately for marketing people, several market research houses have fairly accurate tools for measuring brand acceptance and forecasting demand as a result of simulated marketing. (Test marketing achieves the same things, but it takes a lot longer to measure results.) For example, one company was not sure how price would affect the demand for and the image of its new brand. So acceptance for the brand was measured among two groups of identically matched consumers. All the elements—packaging, product, advertising, and so on—were the same, except for price. The resulting forecasts showed that although the higher-priced offering sold fewer units, it delivered the same

EVERY LASH LONGER OR YOUR MONEY BACK.

If our new Cutex Every Lash Longer Mascara isn't the most fabulous lengthening mascara you've ever tried, we'll gladly refund your money.

It performs exceptionally. The creamy-rich formula dramatically elongates your lashes. While the specially tapered brush clings to and defines even the most elusive little lashes.

It's smudgeproof and smearproof too. So those sweepingly long lush lashes you get last all day or all night. And of course, it's hypoallergenic.

Kindly enclose the used Every Lash Longer Mascara if applying for refund. Write Cutex, P.O. Box 4008, Jefferson City, MO. 65102.

Cutex Perfect Color

revenue. And as might be expected, the image of the brand had a much stronger quality component (the WIFM) at the higher price. It also became apparent that the production department might not be able to keep up with demand at the lower price. The brand was priced at the higher level and has been very successful.

The other practical difficulty in getting all the elements of a brand to work toward the communication of the WIFM is in the selection of the brand's name. Naming a new brand can be a nightmare. Even if you come up with the best name in the world that checks out positively in every piece of consumer research and contributes a full point to the WIFM measurement scale, if the boss doesn't like it, it's back to the drawing board. What happens when you give a brand a name is that for the first time, the brand is given a personality. Up to this point it was merely Formula 431 or the X2K project. All of a sudden the X2K is given an identity. You cannot win on names, because you are dealing with human beings with feelings, and issues that are emotional, not intellectual. What would have happened to the poor brand manager who recommended the name Skippy for a peanut butter if the president's wayward brother was nicknamed Skippy?

In brand-name selection, the best you can do is find a name that is at least neutral. By neutral I mean:

1. It doesn't contribute or detract from your WIFM.
2. It has no unpleasant image associations.
3. It is relatively easy to pronounce.

Brand names have become such a specialized business that consulting companies have sprung up to help marketers choose a name. I don't know what their criteria are, but one I would recommend is, don't call your brand or company Mr./Mister something. Although Mr./Mister was probably intended to communicate that the brand or company was so superior that it deserved a title, Mr./Mister is now so overused that it has become a joke. I've found over a hundred examples so far, including Mister Chop Suey, Mr. Front End, Mr. Jerk (what does he do?), Mr. Travel, and Mister Courier.

Rule 8: No Piggybacking

There is a lot of brand name piggybacking going on today, and it mystifies me: Why do companies use a good brand name for subsegment spin-offs? The principal arguments for piggybacking brand names are that you capture some of the positive imagery of the parent brand and that they are easier for consumers to deal with than new entities with totally new names. That seems to make sense, but if you believe, as I do, that a brand name should communicate the brand WIFM, how can a new brand that has a different WIFM from the parent brand use the same name? How can Miller Lite, a lighter, less filling, lower-calorie brand that tastes different and meets different needs, use the same brand name as Miller regular? The WIFMs are entirely different.

When you borrow a strong name that means something positive and lend it to a new offspring that meets different consumer needs, you are likely to hurt the parent in the process by either confusing the poor consumer or, in some way, modifying the WIFM of the parent brand. The truth is that every beer connoisseur knows that light beer is less of a beer because it has fewer ingredients in it and tastes watered down. To call it Miller Lite seems to me to detract from the parent brand in some way. The piggyback name may work well for the offspring, but the parent gets burned in the process. Miller Lite now outsells Miller High Life. Perhaps this can't be blamed on the name alone. Perhaps the company got so caught up in the success of the baby that it forgot the parent.

There are those in the cigarette and beer industries who believe that when the market is trading down to milder versions of the product category, you should line-extend the name to keep consumers in the same family of brands. In the cigarette business, for example, consumers are moving to light and ultralight brands due to the cancer scare. Therefore, the cigarette companies are creating light and ultralight versions of their regular brands and borrowing the names so consumers will stay within a family of brands as they move lighter.

It's hard to argue against this line of logic, except to point out that the evidence shows that one of the brands has lost market share every time this was done—in most cases, the parent brand. If the cigarette market is moving light, this may not matter, since the parent is going to die anyway. However, to use the cigarette example as justification for line-extending names in almost every other packaged-goods product class is a mistake, since in most brand situations, the marketer cares a lot if the parent gets hurt. And I find it hard to believe that it's just coincidence that Miller High Life and numerous cigarette parent brands have suffered massive share declines when their milder children borrowed their names and imagery.

I praised Palmolive earlier in the book for its coup when it introduced Palmolive automatic liquid dishwashing detergent. Its WIFM was clear and it met an unfulfilled need in the marketplace. No matter how much each powdered dishwashing detergent said otherwise, people knew that powders left a residue on the glasses. But I wish Palmolive had given the brand a name that communicated its WIFM. I'm not very creative when it comes to brand names, but New Sheeting Action Palmolive or New Palmolive Sparkle would have communicated that the brand doesn't leave a residue on dishes. These names would have separated liquids used in dishwashers from liquids used in the sink and from all the other Palmolive soaps out there. These names would also have helped communicate the WIFM, and that's the point of this WIFM rule and the principle of WIFMs— precise communication that tells consumers why your brand meets their needs better than your competitors' brands.

12

The Importance of Proximity

The headline boomed from the November 30, 1987, *Marketing* magazine article: BRAND LOYALTY SLIPPING AMONG CONSUMERS. The article went on to quote the national director of strategic planning for a major advertising agency, who said, "Consumer brand loyalty continues to decline and that can have a major effect on advertising."

I was not surprised to read that brand loyalty was slipping. But I was surprised at the comment that the slippage in brand loyalty can have an effect on advertising, since, in my judgment, much of today's advertising has caused lower brand loyalty, not the other way around.

To be successful, an ad has to strike a chord of emotion in consumers to get registration and to persuade them to purchase. The viewer of a commercial has to become involved with the commercial through either logic or emotion. This is what I mean by *proximity*. But this is what is throwing advertisers and agencies off the WIFM track and into generalized messages, with pretty people doing pretty things in conjunction with hundreds of perfectly good brands and product classes that consumers would like to be loyal to.

I am a strong proponent of the principle of personally touching the consumer with an advertising message and would like to make it a corollary to my WIFM rules, but some clarification is needed first.

When I watch my daughter swoon over a certain baby in a disposable diaper commercial, I have living proof of the need for the ad to touch someone, to have proximity. But when I ask her several minutes later what the brand was, she has trouble remembering. The emotional link between the cuteness of the baby and her maternal instinct was made, but the transference of this emotion to the brand did not occur. Why not? The emotional link has absolutely nothing to do with either the benefits of disposable diapers or the reason someone should buy one brand over another.

Parents buy disposable diapers for their convenience over cloth diapers, and they buy specific brands to meet a host of tangible and intangible product-class and brands needs: cost, leakproofness, absorbency, fit, and comfort. These needs, when met, result in a happy, healthy baby. But a baby can be just as happy and healthy in a cloth diaper. And a baby can be happy because it has just eaten.

Well-meaning advertisers are working backwards: They assume that if you show people the effect, they will automatically assume that the brand was the cause. That's illogical.

Take the case of Kentucky Fried Chicken. When the Colonel was alive, the brand had a living, credible spokesman for its WIFM. The brand stood for a distinctive taste that no one else could duplicate because only the Colonel knew the secret of the spice blend. But after the Colonel died, the brand had a life-style campaign that communicated the warmth and closeness of groups of people that happened to be munching on KFC. I knew that when I saw this ad I was supposed to empathize with the scene and transfer my positive feelings about it to the chicken, but the groups of people in the KFC ads could just as easily have been eating Chinese food or pizza.

Paul Gottlieb said this better than I ever could in his classic April 24, 1989, article from *Marketing*, "The Metaphoric Mode." He too was commenting on the lack of linkage in the two halves of an advertising metaphor:

> Similarities, metaphors and symbols derive much of their
> power from the process of discovery and recognition under-

> gone by the audience.... I believe there is a correlation between an unforced, natural association of two different ideas and the ease with which it is noticed and remembered.

He understands that ads cannot persuade, let alone register the advertiser's name, if the link isn't made between the metaphor and what the brand stands for in consumers' minds.

Finding a Metaphorical Link

I have always been intrigued with the idea of brand personalities as a brand-positioning device. But I have learned through experience that the technique can't be applied in very many cases. Unfortunately, some advertising agencies are so enamored of the technique that they try to apply it to every brand in their stable. I think many of them do this because brand personalities not only seem to deliver a plausible message, they cast and set a commercial simultaneously. Who wouldn't be attracted to something that does the entire job for you?

Some brands decide to use Badge Theory/Brand Personality Theory positioning for what sounds like a good marketing reason but, when examined logically, isn't: The brand's image is old and tired. It seems to make sense that if your market research reveals that consumers perceive your brand as old and tired, you should change the image of the brand by showing young, contemporary people in your commercials. This is, however, a terrible mistake that marketers make every day when they use Badge Theory illogic. Most times, life-style advertising shows the types of people the marketer would *like* to have consuming the brand.

We used to do this in the beer business until one day we discovered that every brand in our category (ours and our competitors') that was losing market share was characterized by consumers as old and tired, and all the brands that were growing were considered to be young and vibrant. It didn't matter what brand it was, if it was on the down side of the life-cycle curve, its user image was of drinkers who were set in their ways and so old that pretty soon they would all die off and the brand would be left appealing to no one. But the fact that a brand's image was inextricably tied to its position on the life-cycle curve is the clue that tells the marketer that this is a product class phenomenon, not a brand issue. This should lead back to the brand issue—superiority—and away from expecting that product class, people-type advertising showing young people using the brand will change the brand's image.

Ask yourself a logical question before embarking on a brand-revitalization strategy using people-type brand positioning alone: Historically, did the advertising show old, tired people using the brand, giving the brand this image in the first place? Chances are the answer is no. So why would you assume that showing young, vibrant people using the brand will somehow turn the brand's image around? That's Brand Personality/Badge Theory illogic that doesn't link the two halves of the metaphor.

Old, tired brands got old, tired user images because the marketer didn't change the product, or the package, or the advertising, or other elements of the marketing mix to keep up with the times. People who wanted to keep up with the times moved to another brand that offered them contemporary values that kept pace with their needs.

When this happens the marketer is left with few strategic options. Virtually everything that has been done in the past must be changed. Just changing the brand's outward appearance—the "image" components such as packaging and advertising—is a very weak response when the competition is claiming that it does best what the product class was supposed to do in the first place. The consumer is still left saying, "Okay, I know you want me to think your brand is more contemporary by showing contemporary people consuming it and by changing the packaging to make it look more up to date, but why does any of that make your product superior to the leading brand? It has had contemporary advertising and packaging for a long time. When I look around I see lots of contemporary people consuming their product. What have you done to make your product better?"

Delivering an Exclusive Message

I have been accused over the years of being against life-style advertising. This is true only to the extent that I am against the mindless use of people types if they do not support or represent the brand's WIFM in any way. There is a place for people-type positioning at the product-class level and, therefore, there is a place for life-style advertising. However, day after day, we see almost the same visuals for different brands in different product classes. What do the visuals have to do with the superiority of one brand over another? If the advertiser doesn't have an *exclusive message*—one that only its brand in the product class can claim (the reason for the brand's superiority)—all it is doing is advertising the merits of the product class or the merits of several product classes. All it says to consumers is, "I am here."

Proof of this statement is in the demonstration. For example, take the October 19, 1989, edition of *Time* magazine and look at each ad. Out of the fifty-two advertisers that bought a half-page ad or larger, only eight had WIFM ads—roughly 15 percent. The remaining 85 percent were ads that chose to communicate the general virtues of the product class despite very strong competition from brands within the immediate product class and/or strong competition from other product classes. In every case, the needs that these advertisers were laying claim to were so general that they could cover hundreds of brands in hundreds of product classes.

The old dictum that 50 percent of advertising is wasted, but no one knows which half, is incorrect. If this one issue of *Time* magazine is any indication, it's more likely that 85 percent of advertising is wasted, and WIFMs are the way to determine which 85 percent.

The Allure of Badge Theory

The other day, I passed three almost identical billboards for three different brands of jeans. All had a bluish tint to them, all had a very shapely young woman's bottom dominating the visual, and all had a svelte young man's bottom in close proximity to the woman's. None of the brands told us why it was superior to the competition. Indeed, the opposite was true: They all told us that they were so similar that it really didn't matter which one we chose. Why would advertising agencies and clients allow this to happen? Wasn't each manufacturer upset when it saw the competitors' ads?

Then another copy of *Marketing* magazine came across my desk that contained one plausible answer. A headline in the November 2, 1987, issue stated: ADVERTISING SHOULD BE CHARMING, SEDUCTIVE. In essence, the message (and it's a valid point) was that the consumer is bombarded with so many ads in one day that an ad must be imaginative, charming, and seductive to make it stand apart from the crowd. Those blue jean billboards certainly caught my attention. They were imaginative, charming, and especially seductive. But they didn't tell me about the superiority of one brand over another.

Clutter

When you watch one hour of TV, you see roughly twelve minutes of ads. You are exposed to advertising 20 percent of the time. Since each ad is usually thirty seconds long, that means you are exposed to twenty-four ads in an hour. With the advent of fifteen-second commercials, plus a couple of stations breaks and the usual disruption in the middle of a run of commercials to tell you "We will return to our program after the following words from our sponsors," you get roughly thirty messages in an hour, usually clustered in fours or fives. The amount of clutter is incredible, and the accepted solution seems to be life-style advertising.

Art and Advertising

Another problem is that advertising is considered an art form. The art of advertising is its wonderful ability to take something as mundane as a dirty shirt collar and make it so exciting it becomes a household phrase: RING AROUND THE COLLAR. There is a lot of room for art in advertising, which is what many call selling the sizzle along with the steak.

I agree that you have to sell the sizzle along with the steak to cut through the clutter, but I don't agree that you should sell the sizzle for any old brand. This brings up a new WIFM corollary: If an ad looks more like art than advertising, it probably *is* art rather than advertising.

The ads pictured here are from competing companies in the travel industry: one for an airline, Cathay Pacific, and the other for a cruise ship, the Royal Caribbean. Both have the sizzle (the beautiful pictures), but only one has a WIFM.

I was attracted to the Cathay Pacific ad because I love antiques and places with a long history, and I love San Francisco. But the ad doesn't have a WIFM. Moreover, there is no direct link between the visuals and the brand. When I got through reading it, my reaction was, I could get there just as easily using another airline. Why should I take Cathay Pacific?

I have flown on Cathay Pacific, and it is a wonderful flying experience. There are lots of potential WIFMs it could have used to convey its superiority to the competition. For example, its attention to detail in pampering customers is outstanding—so good, in fact, that it doesn't even have to offer a frequent-flier plan to compete effectively. But consumers won't know about Cathay Pacific's superiority if it tells them only that it flies to a certain location.

Of course, it's important for an airline to let people know what its routes are. In this case, San Francisco was a new route for Cathay Pacific, and creating awareness was the goal of the advertising. However, Cathay had strong competition from at least two other airlines on that route. After reading the ad, the consumer now knows that Cathay flies to San Francisco. But for those travelers who haven't experienced Cathay's pampering, there is still no reason to choose Cathay over the competition. Cathay could have strengthened its advertisement by closing the loop from awareness of the new route to WIFMs by stating the reasons for its superiority over the competition on that route.

The Royal Caribbean ad is a perfect example of the old adage that every problem is an opportunity in disguise. Most travel ads don't have WIFMs. They all show pretty pictures, usually of scantily clad women running on beautiful wide stretches of white beach. But how can you figure out why one packaged vacation is better than another when the visuals and the messages are interchangeable?

It isn't France. But you're close.

Tiny inns nestle in leafy lanes. Vineyards offer laden branches to the sun.
In California. Cathay Pacific's California. Discover how close.
Just two hours away. Discover how reasonable.
And discover the unique travelling experience of Cathay Pacific's luxurious 747
International Service from Vancouver to San Francisco.
For further information, ask your Travel Agent
for the brochure entitled "Sanfrantastic Holidays."

Discover Cathay Pacific's California.

Arrive in better shape.

Royal Caribbean shows the same beautiful scene that every other travel ad does, but it has turned the sameness of all the other ads to its advantage. A sunset is a sunset, but a sunset viewed from a Royal Caribbean ship is better because of the long list of brand values Royal Caribbean provides. This ad was a piece of art, but for the first time in a travel ad, the art was tied to a message, and the reason for buying this brand over someone else's was clear.

High Wear-Out

The third reason that a lot of advertisers use Badge Theory so extensively rather than WIFMs is that ads are so expensive to create and run. Wear-out becomes critical. For example, as part of some market research, consumers were shown a commercial that hadn't been run for over two years. Yet every one of the focus group members mentioned how sick they were of seeing the commercial. That's wear-out.

In explaining why TV advertising has become a reminder medium, the respected creative director Paul Gottlieb made the following statement in the October 5, 1987, issue of *Marketing* magazine:

> Having to pass the endurance test of high frequency, high repeat viewership and high production costs, it is quite natural that commercials aim to entertain. Naturally, no matter how good the track, how vivid the video, ultimately the commercials tend to wear out. Especially in such product categories as beer, where the majority of brands could still exchange bottles or cans with one another, without anyone noticing any appreciable difference in visual content or treatment.

There can be no doubt that wear-out, like clutter, is a real issue, but neither wear-out, clutter, nor the art of advertising—nor the weight of all three combined—should ever be used to justify the use of Badge Theory, Brand Personality Theory, or life-style advertising over WIFM advertising.

(Text continued on page 194.)

Why Our Sunset Is

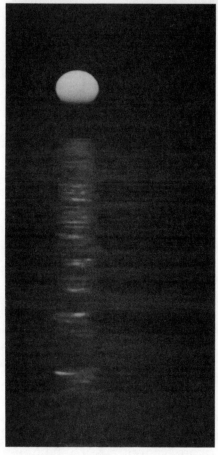

Substance vs. Style

Make no mistake about it: Whether to use Badge Theory advertising or WIFM advertising is a style-versus-substance issue. But
good WIFM ads must blend substance with style in today's
advertising environment to be successful. The lack of substance
results in reminder advertising, and the lack of style results in
boring, nonimpacting advertising. In my opinion, however, it is
usually better to err on the side of lack of style than lack of
substance.

One of my favorite WIFM ads is the one from Q-tips. This
ad proves that the advertiser can combine the sizzle with the
steak and produce a motivating advertisement that has proximity. The simplicity of the ad makes it stand out from the clutter of
other ads in a magazine that was just loaded with them. And
Q-tips' softness WIFM is beautifully demonstrated in the visual.
Softness is a value-added brand WIFM that makes Q-tips superior to its competition and a good, solid reason for the consumer
to buy the brand.

In the case of the Fabergé Organics ad, the blending of the
girl's hair into the wheat field is excellent support for the brand's
purity WIFM and a nice blend of substance and style.

The Proper Use of Life-Style Advertising

Many who use "image" advertising forget three important things:

1. Most images (occasions-for-use, user personalities, life-
   styles, moods, and so on) are at the product class, not
   the brand level.
2. Product-class needs, as depicted by life-style advertising,
   are often so general that they apply to a multiplicity of
   product classes and, therefore, cannot possibly be trans-
   ferable to only one brand, let alone only one product
   class.
3. The image will transfer to a specific brand only if the link
   is made between the need and a brand's superiority in
   meeting that need. That territory is most often reserved
   for the brand leader or a trade association.

Don't you wish the whole world were as pure and natural as the wheat germ oil and honey in Fabergé Organics Shampoo?

For natural shine and natural body that can make a world of difference in your hair.

CONTAINS NATURAL AND OTHER INGREDIENTS.

Fabergé Organics with pure Wheat Germ Oil & Honey Shampoo

Badge Theory/Brand Personality brand positioning cannot be used for establishing WIFMs, therefore, unless brand superiority can be established and demonstrated at the product-class level. Once this is done, the marketer has moved into the effective use of *true brand personalities* and can use life-style advertising to communicate the WIFM.

Evidence That True Brand Personalities Work

I recently had the opportunity to empirically test the Brand Personality/Badge Theory brand-positioning issues and examine the differences between Badge Theory and true brand personalities. In this particular piece of market research in the refreshment beverage category, we put a series of both people-type measurements (measures of basic human needs, occasions for use, life-styles, and demographics) and brand values in one questionnaire. The output from this combination of research items was incredible. At the product-class level, we found certain needs and personality characteristics that pertained to every brand in the category—the price-of-entry needs that every brand in the category must meet to be considered a serious player. Such consumer needs as thirst quenching and refreshment were quickly identified as important ingredients in the selection of any brand in this product class. These needs linked up nicely with summer occasions for use and certain life-style scenarios, such as just lazing around with a few casual friends in the afternoon. The sociability and casual fun of the occasions also linked up nicely with one major personality characteristic associated with drinkers of this product class: hedonism.

Normally, when researchers use rating scales in a research study (brand-value scales, life-style scales, personality scales, or whatever), there are so many scales that it is easiest to group the various scales (individual ideas) together to form concepts. A mathematical technique called *factor analysis* is usually employed, and that's what we did in this study. For example, individual personality items such as self-indulgence, living life to the fullest, and being good to oneself were linked by factor analysis to form the group of ideas that we nicknamed hedonism. As usual, we factored the people-type rating scales separately from the brand values and reduced our 150 scales to twenty meaningful and explainable concepts. The researcher's task, at this stage, is to look at the factors and give them simple names that capture the common idea of the factor or concept. After I did this, I realized that I had given the same name to certain factors in the people section and in the brand-values section. Then it hit me that the proof of True Brand Personality Theory (as opposed to Badge Theory) was right before my eyes: *In true brand personalities, people types are just a substitute for the brand value.* In other words, to give a brand a certain personality automatically implies that the brand delivers certain benefits.

To test this, I mixed the people and brand-value statements together and refactored them. The link was made between personalities and brand values for certain items. For example, our new "quality" factor contained both types of items:

Brand Value	*People Type*
Classy/elegant image	Tries to buy the best
Can serve it with pride	Demands quality
Made with care	Refined and cultured
Impresses people	A connoisseur

I had hypothesized for years that you could substitute brand values for people types metaphorically, but this was my first opportunity to prove that it was possible to establish a direct link.

Since the client's brand best met consumer needs for quality and thirst quenching, it could use brand personalities to communicate its WIFM. The metaphor can work, but only if there is a direct cause-and-effect link between the two pieces of the metaphor. The cause (the client's brand) met consumer needs for thirst quenching and quality better than every brand in the product class, and consumers knew this. Therefore, the effect (hedonistic people enjoying the brand on hot-weather occasions) could be logically deduced from the cause. To cement the link, the client's advertising told consumers the brand values that made the brand meet consumer needs better than the competition.

That's proximity: communicating a WIFM in such a way that it touches people emotionally because the brand's WIFM is a direct cause of the consumer's emotional state. Without proximity, there is no brand-name registration, and there is nothing for the consumer to be loyal to.

I can now say that I am definitely not against life-style advertising *if* the life-style depicted or the personality of the brand that you want to communicate can be tied directly to the brand's superiority claim. The Marlboro man is a good example of what I mean. The brand's WIFM is strong taste, which it supports with a rugged individual in all its ads. The strength of the taste of the brand is clearly communicated by the cowboy on the horse.

Back to WIFM Basics

Fabergé, Q-tips, and the other WIFM advertisers mentioned in this book have not forgotten the basics of WIFM marketing:

- Consumers are intelligent individuals who have wants and needs for your brands.
- Consumers are constantly seeking information about brands or services that will help make their lives a little better.
- Consumers will be receptive to your message as long as they are told why they should buy in their terms, not your terms.
- You enter into a partnership with consumers when you deliver a superior product or service that meets their needs, and this partnership will exist forever as long as you continue to serve their needs better than anyone else.

Most of all, remember that brand advertising targets at needs, not people, and people do not need advertising to entertain them. Advertising's role is to motivate. Following the WIFM rules brings marketers back to this important truth.

WIFMs do not stifle creativity—just the opposite. As demonstrated by many of the excellent WIFM ads in this book, WIFMs force creative directors to reach higher. Only then will there be a satisfactory two-way relationship of mutual respect between the advertiser and the consumer. Only then will the marketer truly understand what customer-driven brand positionings are.

Index

Achievers, 49, 50, 60
advertising, 5
  art and, 188–191
  emotional appeal of, 183–184
  emotional needs in, 72–73
  formula for, 27–29, 158–159
  imprecision in, 37–39
  of product class, 76, 80–82
  production costs of, 73
  showing benefits to consumer, 35–37
  superiority of, 110–111
  that makes consumer work hard, 35–36
  that merely creates awareness, 78–79
  that not even creates awareness, 79–82
  see also TV advertising
after-use factors, superiority of, 103–104
Ajax cleanser ad, superiority claim of, 14
Alive and Well, customer-oriented approach of, 32–33
Amstrad ad, occasion-for-use theme of, 58–59
audience measurement service, 63

awareness
  creation of, 78–79
  failure to create, 79–82

Babe perfume, esteem needs in marketing of, 57
Badge Theory, 70–75, 94, 159
  allure of, 187–191
  in cola wars, 112–113
  improper use of, 78, 197
  versus true brand personality, 197–199
  used by brand leader, 91–92
Basic Stance, 17–20
Beatrice Corporation, corporate slogan of, 127
Beefeater ad, brand-name confusion in, 79–82
beer advertising, 77–78, 135
"before-and-after" advertising formula, 27–29
belonging, need for, 22–23
benefits
  advertising that describes, 36
  consumers' vs. marketers' concern about, 39–41
  derived, 65–67
  and life-style segment, 49–50

benefits (*continued*)
  versus needs, 37–41
  owning of, 157–158
brand-blind product tests, 115, 116
brand leadership, 91–92
brand loyalty, 183
brand names, 180
  piggybacking of, 181–182
brand needs, 30
brand personalities, effective use
  of, 194, 197–199
Brand Personality Theory, 78, 94
brand positioning, 1–3, 141–146,
  142–144
  based on customer needs, 30
  by Basic Stance/USP system,
    18–26
  brands vs. product classes in,
    69–83
  Cannibalization Factor in, 52–53
  Chicken Approach to, 53–55
  conforming tactics and, 147–148
  life-style, 48–50
  Marketing Warfare, 89–91
  to narrow target group, 44–48
  people-type theory in, 63–64
  by WIFM system, 26–31
brands, 68
  acceptance of, 178–180
  all needs in strategy for, 56–67
  Basic Stance for, 17–20
  consumer benefits of, 171–175
  contributing elemenets of, to
    success, 148–149
  differentiation of, 69
  finding metaphorical link for,
    185–186
  humanizing of, 72–73
  "ideal," 137–140
  modification of, 52–54
  monopoly of, 91
  personality of, 70–72
  versus product classes, 68–83
  ratings of, 140–141
  wrong strategy for, 63–64
brand-selection criteria, 135–137,
  142, 167–171
brand value needs, 56, 62, 82–83
brand WIFMs, 95–119, 132

Cannibalization Factor, 52–53
Cathay Pacific ads, art of, 189, 190
Chicken Approach, 53–54
Chrysler
  competitive strategies of, 166
  corporate image problems of,
    125–126
  superiority of, 97
clones, 153–157
Close-Up ad, multiple WIFMs in,
  171, 172
clutter, 188
Coca Cola, advertising strategy of,
  112–114, 116
Cola Wars, 111–114, 117
Colgate, toothpaste pump
  dispenser of, 159–164
Colonial cookies ad, value claim
  of, 169–171
company mission, 131
competition, 69–70, 76, 94
  weakness of, 89–93
  wise, 175–178
competitive corporate deficiencies,
  126–127
conforming tactics, 147–148
Conservatives, 60
consumer, 4–5, 118–119
  brand attributes and benefits for,
    171–175
  categorization of, 73–74
  distance of, 33–35
  listening to, 117–119
  listening to vs. telling, 18–19

perception of, 1–3
rapport with, 15
seeing product through eyes of, 29–30, 32–41
treating, with dignity and trust, 32–33
trends in, 149–150
consumer action statement, 4
consumer information, 3
consumer needs, 17, 20–26, 30, 42–55
and brand value needs, 82–83
versus corporate needs, 51–55
tuning in to, 35–37
understanding of, 34–35
see also specific needs
consumer verification, 131–141
Continental tire ad, consumer benefits in, 171–175
Cooper, Robert (*Winning at New Products*), on reasons for product successes and failures, 156–157
Coors beer, superiority of, 97
corporate image statement, variables in, 120–121
corporate needs, 51–55
corporate slogans, 127–128
corporate WIFMs, 120–128
corporation
deficiencies of, 124–127
legitimate superiority of, 123–124
creativity, 199–200
customer, *see* consumer
customer-driven companies, 34–35
customer-oriented approach, 32–33
customer service, superiority of, 102–103
Cutex Every Lash Longer mascara ad, continuity of elements in, 178

demographic needs, 57
demographic segment, 42–50
demonstrability, 153–159
derived benefits, 65–67
discounting, 105
Dow Chemical, corporate image problems of, 125
Downy fabric softener, Derived Benefit of, 65–66
Dow's Saran Wrap ad, superiority claim of, 14–15

ease of use, for consumer, 102–103
emotional needs, 58–60, 72–73
environment, and human needs, 57
environmental friendliness, 38–39, 105
esteem needs, 24–25, 57
exclusive message, 186–187
Exxon, oil-spill problems of, 125

Fabergé Organics ad, substance vs. style in, 194, 196
factor analysis, 197–198
Federal Express, superiority of, 97
focus groups, 137–138, 140–141, 147–148
following the followers, 53–55
Ford
competitive strategies of, 166
corporate image problems of, 125–126
forecasting, 23–24, 178–180

General Motors, corporate WIFM of, 124
Gillette, twin-blade cartridges of, 156
Goodrich ad, tying attributes to consumer benefits, 175, 176–177

Gottlieb, Paul
    on power of metaphor, 184–185
    on TV commercials, 5, 191
grey market, 46
Guinness beer, packaging of, 101

healthiness, superiority of, 105
Honda, creative ads of, 159,
    160–161
human needs, hierarchy of, 20–26,
    57
Hunter fan ad, superiority claim
    of, 14

Iacocca, Lee, turning around of
    Chrysler by, 166
IBM, track record of, 156
"ideal" brand, determination of,
    137–140
image advertising, 194–197
image problems, 125–126
image products, 111–114
Innovators, 49, 60

Jaguar ad, 162–163
Jif peanut butter ad, superiority
    claim of, 14
John Labatt Classic beer, target
    group for, 43–44

Kao Soap Company
    marketing strategy of, 6–7
    percentage of employees in
        R&D, 34
    product preference for, 115
Kentucky Fried Chicken, life-style
    campaign of, 184
Kitty Litter Brand, WIFM in, 84–85
Kobe beef, superiority of, 50
Kohn, Paul, beer ad study of,
    77–78

Kraft Parmesan ad, superiority in,
    97, 99

leadership stance, 91–92, 110–111,
    151
life-cycle theory, 49
life-style
    needs of, 60
    research on, 73–75
    TV viewing patterns and, 63–64
life-style positioning, 19–20, 48–50,
    184–185, 194–197
life-style segmentation, 47–48, 49,
    73–74
love needs, 22–24

manufacturers, customer distance
    problem for, 34–35
market
    appeal to heart of, 165–167
    dominance of, 165
    monitoring of, 149–150
market-expansion stance, 151
marketing
    basics of, 3–5, 199–200
    budget for, 105–106
    simplicity of, 3
marketing-warfare stance, 151
market leaders
    finding vulnerability of, 175–178
    variation of, 23–24
market research, 23–24, 131–141,
    147, 148–149
    basics of, 135–137
    quantitative-qualitative, 140–141
market segmentation, 16, 68–69,
    93–94, 136
Maslow, Abraham, hierarchy of
    needs theory of, 20–26
Mennen's baby oil ad, superiority
    claim of, 8–14

message
   determination of first, 50–51
   exclusive, 186–187
metaphor
   effectiveness of, 184–185, 198
   misuse of, 79–80
metaphorical link, 185–186
me-too brands, 107, 153–157
Miller Lite
   market research on, 138
   piggybacking of, 181
   popularity of, 104–105
   risk reduction ad for, 87
Miracle Whip ad, before-and-after
   approach in, 27–28

needs, 37–39, 50–51, 56–67, 66, 80,
   135
   versus benefits, 37–41
   brand, 56, 62
   corporate vs. consumer, 51–55
   emotional, 37
   ideal vs. actual satisfaction of,
      139
   interaction of, 62–63
   people, 56, 57–61
   targeting of, 42–55
   see also consumer needs; human
      needs, hierarchy of
new-category stance, 151
new-product strategy, 156–157
New Values consumer, 60
niche stance, 151–152
nonreproducibility, 159–164

occasion-for-use needs, 57–58
Oxy Clean ad sequence, brand
   WIFMs in, 133–134

packaging, superiority of, 101–102
paired comparison, 115

Palmolive dishwashing detergents
   market research on, 138
   me-too of, 154
   piggybacking of, 182
peer acceptance, 22–23
people needs, 56, 57–61, 66, 82–83
   market research in, 135–136
people-type brand positioning,
      185–186
   flaws of, 74–75
people-type rating scales, 197–198
Pepsi, advertising strategy of,
   113–114, 116
Perrier, filter problems of, 125
personal message, 37
physiological needs, 21
piggybacking, 181–182
popularity, as WIFM, 104–105
Positioning (Ries and Trout), on
      competing wisely, 175
positioning map, 142–146
positioning stances, 150–152
precise communication, 37–39
price
   reductions of, 105–108
   testing of, 148
Procter & Gamble, Jif peanut
      butter ad of, 14
product
   acceptance of, 117
   easy-to-buy, 4
   high failure rate of, 3
   superiority of, 27–29, 97–101
   testing of, 114–116
   uniqueness of, 16–17
product classes, 8, 76, 136
   versus brands, 68–83
   competition in, 69–70
   definition of, 68, 131–133
   emotion created by, 60
   hurting sales of, 76–78

product classes (*continued*)
   identification of consumers who
      use, 50–51
   minimum standards in, 86
   needs satisfied by, 57–58
   primary demand for, 92
   redefinition of, 87–89
product-class needs, 30, 130
product-class WIFMs, 84–94
promotions, 105–108
   audits of, 108–110
proximity, importance of, 183–200
psychographic market research,
      48–49, 60
public esteem, 24

Q-tips ad, substance vs. style in,
      194, 195
quality, 64
quantitative-qualitative market
      research, 140–141
Quorum ad, brand personality in,
      70–72

retailing, customer distance in,
      33–34
retail outlets, branding of, 123
Ries, Al (*Positioning*), 175
risk-reduction stance, 151
risks, 86–87
   reduction of, 87, 93
Royal Caribbean ad, WIFM in,
      189–193

safety needs, 22
Saran Wrap, superiority claim of,
      14–15
Schlitz beer, taste superiority claim
      of, 115–116
seasonality, 136
self-actualization, 22, 25–26
self-esteem, 24–25

sensory superiority, 157, 158–159
service companies, customer
      distance in, 34
socio-geo-demographic needs, 57
standards, minimum, 86
substance-style issue, 6–7, 194
Suisse Mocha ad, sugar-free, 89–90
Sunlight dishwashing detergent
      ad, 58–61
superiority, 8–15, 27–29, 84, 96–111
   corporate, 123–124
   positioning in terms of, 20
   in product, 17, 97–101
   product-class WIFM as, 92–93
   sensory, 157, 158–159
Suzuki Sidekick, defect of, 127

target group, 46–47, 147–148
   mistake of selecting first, 42–50
   narrowing of, 44–48, 65–66
   wrong, 43–44
taste tests, 115–116
Taurus, consumer market research
      on, 166–167
tracking results, 149–150
track record, 154–156
Trout, Jack (*Positioning*), 175
True Brand Personality Theory,
      197–199
TV advertising
   clutter in, 188
   high frequency of, 191
   lack of corporate WIFMs on, 124
   lack of message in, 5
TV viewing, life-styles and, 63–64

Unique Selling Proposition (USP)
      theory, 16–17, 72, 107
uniqueness, 16–17

value-added characteristics, 62

"value" excuse, for extra WIFMs, 169–171
variety, as product superiority, 103
Virginia Slims cigarettes, niche of, 57
Volvo ad, superiority in, 97, 98

wear-out, high level of, 191
WIFM positioning stances, 150–152
WIFMs, 48–50, 86–91
  appealing to heart of market with, 165–167
  basics of, 199–200
  brand, 95–119
  consumer verification of, 131–141
  continuity of elements of, 178–180
  corporate, 120–128
  definition and examples of, 8–31
  demonstrability of, 153–159
  determining message of first, 50–51
  in-house data on, 131
  nonreproducibility of, 159–164
  owning of, 157–158
  people-type, 62

piggybacking of, 181–182
positioning of, 153–182
product-class, 84–94
search for, 129–152
use of, one at a time, 167–171
WIFM system, 6–7, 18–20, 27–29, 129–130, 131, 147–148
  basics of, 29–31
  versus Basic Stance/USP theory, 26
  brand positioning in, 141–146
  consumer perception in, 2–3
  market research in, 131–141, 148–149
  tracking results in, 149–150
Wilkinson Sword, twin-blade cartridge, 154–156
Winning at New Products (Cooper), on product success factors, 156–157
Wiser's ad, superiority in, 97, 100

Xerox, confusion of brand with corporation, 122

Yuppies, 46, 63–64